ISLANDS OF THE DAMNED

R. V. Burgin

WITH BILL MARVEL

ISLANDS OF THE DAMNED

A MARINE AT WAR IN THE PACIFIC

NAL
CALIBER

NAL Caliber
Published by New American Library, a division of
Penguin Group (USA) Inc., 375 Hudson Street,
New York, New York 10014, USA
Penguin Group (Canada), 90 Eglinton Avenue East, Suite 700, Toronto,
Ontario M4P 2Y3, Canada (a division of Pearson Penguin Canada Inc.)
Penguin Books Ltd., 80 Strand, London WC2R 0RL, England
Penguin Ireland, 25 St. Stephen's Green, Dublin 2,
Ireland (a division of Penguin Books Ltd.)
Penguin Group (Australia), 250 Camberwell Road, Camberwell, Victoria 3124,
Australia (a division of Pearson Australia Group Pty. Ltd.)
Penguin Books India Pvt. Ltd., 11 Community Centre, Panchsheel Park,
New Delhi—110 017, India
Penguin Group (NZ), 67 Apollo Drive, Rosedale, North Shore 0632,
New Zealand (a division of Pearson New Zealand Ltd.)
Penguin Books (South Africa) (Pty.) Ltd., 24 Sturdee Avenue,
Rosebank, Johannesburg 2196, South Africa

Penguin Books Ltd., Registered Offices:
80 Strand, London WC2R 0RL, England

First published by NAL Caliber, an imprint of New American Library,
a division of Penguin Group (USA) Inc.

First Printing, March 2010
10 9 8 7 6 5 4 3 2

LIBRARY OF CONGRESS CATALOGING-IN-PUBLICATION DATA:

Burgin, R. V.
Islands of the Damned: A Marine at War in the Pacific/R. V. Burgin with Bill Marvel.
p. cm.
ISBN 978-0-451-22990-8
1. Burgin, R. V.   2. World War, 1939–1945—Campaigns—Pacific Area.   3. World War, 1939–1945—Personal
narratives, American.   4. United States. Marine Corps. Regiment, 5th. Battalion, 3rd   5. United States. Marine
Corps—Biography.   6. Marines—United States—Biography.   I. Marvel, Bill.   II. Title.
D769.3725th .B87 2010
940.54'5973092—dc22
[B]   2009040454

Set in Warnock Pro
Designed by Alissa Amell

Printed in the United States of America

PUBLISHER'S NOTE
While the author has made every effort to provide accurate telephone numbers and Internet addresses at the time of
publication, neither the publisher nor the author assumes any responsibility for errors, or for changes that occur after
publication. Further, publisher does not have any control over and does not assume any responsibility for author or
third-party Web sites or their content.

Dedicated to the men in K Company, Third Battalion, Fifth Marine Regiment, First Marine Division—in K/3/5—who fought so valiantly in World War II.

Contents

Luck

I was born on the thirteenth of August, 1922.

My dad was born May 13, 1890.

His brothers, my twin uncles Romus and Remus, were born November 13, 1894. I was named after Romus.

I joined the U.S. Marines on the thirteenth day of November, 1942.

And a big "13" was painted on the side of the amtrac we were about to climb aboard that September morning in 1944, somewhere in the southwest Pacific. It was one of seventeen amtracs tucked into the bay of LST 661, anchored off the coast of a place none of us had ever heard of before—Peleliu.

Motors were gunning, pumping out stinking clouds of blue smoke when we climbed down the ladder into the cramped hold. After a morning up top washed by a steady sea breeze, our eyes burned. Below, it was close and hot as hell. We were burdened with combat packs, carbines, sidearms, first aid kits, KA-BAR knives, two canteens each, struggling to keep a foothold on the pitching deck. NCOs were barking orders into the racket:

"First platoon, load!"

"Second platoon, load!"

"Third platoon, load!"

"Mortar section, load!"

That was us: First Marine Division, Fifth Regiment, Third Battalion, K Company mortars—K/3/5 for short. Two mortars, six men each, two squad leaders, a sergeant and a lieutenant. I was a corporal in charge of one of our 60mm mortars.

Someone spotted the number on the side of the amtrac.

"Jesus! Thirteen. Now we're in the shit."

"Don't worry, boys," I said. "Thirteen's my lucky number."

I believed I was going to come back in one piece. There were guys I knew, Marines I fought alongside, who got a feeling their time was up. Once they got it you couldn't talk them out of it. When we had been fighting to hang on to Walt's Ridge on New Britain, Lonnie Howard said, "Burgin, if anything happens to me, I want you to take my watch."

"You're crazy," I told him. "You'll be okay. Nothing's going to happen to you."

That night one of our artillery shells hit nearby. The shrapnel killed Howard and another Marine, Robert McCarthy.

Me, I was anxious and wary that morning off Peleliu. But I never thought for a minute I wouldn't make it.

Number 13 was one of the older amtracs, the ones without a drop-down back end. When we rolled up on the beach we'd have to scramble over the sides. That's when the Japs would have a clear shot at us. That didn't seem so lucky.

There were about twenty of us, plus the driver, probably a Navy man, all jammed together like toes in a shoe. While we waited, sailors topside looked us over, giving us the thumbs-up and shouting encouragement that we couldn't hear over the noise. Finally the big clamshell doors of that LST—Landing Ship, Tank—cranked open. Number 13 shuddered, and we followed the other amtracs down the ramp, nosed into the water, and floated out into the bright morning sun.

It was a little past eight o'clock.

An amtrac at sea wallows like a buffalo. The flat-bottomed Higgins boats could do twelve knots. We barely managed four and a half, which is about as fast as a man can walk. Think of us walking to shore under fire. We circled for half an hour until the beach master dropped his red flag, the signal to form up and head for shore. Our battleships and cruisers had been working over the island since dawn, guns cracking like thunder. They paused long enough for the Dauntless dive-bombers and TBMs to sweep in and dump their bombs. Then they started up again. After our wave got under way, a couple LSTs that were parked out on our flanks sent swarms of rockets screeching over our heads. I'd never heard a sound like that before. Something like cloth ripping. A curtain of black smoke hung over the whole beach. It looked like the island was on fire.

Somewhere along our way in Jap artillery found the range and started working us over. The last thousand yards we were under fire the whole way. Over the general racket I couldn't hear bullets dinging Number 13, but we kept our heads down anyway. Shells were smacking the water all around us, raising big spikes of foam. Here and there other LSTs and Higgins boats would disappear in a roar of flame. The first bodies floated by. We'd see many more.

About seven hundred yards out, Number 13 lurched and halted, pitching us into one another. Treads flailed and something went grinding and scraping beneath our hull. We'd struck a reef. Now the Jap shells were landing closer—left, right and behind us. We sat there churning the water, and minutes seemed to drag by, though I'm sure only seconds were passing.

Our sergeant, Johnny Marmet, leaned forward and stuck his .45 in the driver's face.

"If you don't get this son of a bitch moving, I'm going to by God shoot you in the head!" he shouted. "We're sitting ducks out here!"

The driver was pushing and pulling controls like a madman, trying to rock a car out of the mud. Treads were spinning, kicking up spray. Then something gently lifted us and we were moving again.

The instant we broke free, an explosion ripped the water right in front of us, dousing us with spray.

I made a quick mental calculation. All that time we'd been moving toward the shore, some Jap gunner was watching us, leading his target. When he figured the trajectory of his shell would intersect our path, he fired. The seconds we'd hung up on that reef were just long enough. If we'd been plowing forward we'd have ended up just where he calculated. That shell would have landed in our laps.

None of us talked about it afterward. We were busy with other things. But I honestly believed it then, and I believe it today. That was a God thing that hung us up on that reef.

_____

We'd been lucky back on Cape Gloucester, too. The Japs expected us, but not where we landed, and we went ashore almost unnoticed and unopposed.

At Peleliu they were waiting for us and they hit us with everything they had. After we stalled on the reef they never gave us a moment's rest. We never felt safe and we never let down our guard, not even for a minute, until the day we left the island.

Number 13 rolled up onto the beach and we bailed over the sides, dropped to the sand and took off running. That's Marine doctrine: Get off the beach. You're a target. You're cluttering things up. Move out!

Beyond the beach lay a strip of dense scrub and, two hundred yards beyond, the enemy airfield that was our first day's objective. A wall of steep hills covered with dense scrub arose behind the airfield. Navy guns were pouring shells into the far edge of the airfield and the high ground beyond, laying in white phosphorous smoke to screen our landing. There was no breeze, and it hung in the air, drifting back over the beach and mingling with black smudge from amtracs and DUKWs burning in the surf.

Coming in, we'd seen our own men floating in the water. Now we came upon the bodies of the Japs who had been caught in the bombardment before we landed. And the body parts. We also saw shell casings, Marine helmets, combat packs, weapons lost or discarded. All battlegrounds eventually look like trash dumps. As the temperature climbed past a hundred, we started dumping things ourselves. The gas masks were the first to go. Then our canvas leggings. They were a nuisance, hot and chafing. Most of us hated them. Later in the day I came upon a bazooka on the ground and I knew exactly who had left it. A bazooka weighed about twenty-four pounds, and he didn't want to carry it. I caught up with him a little farther along and handed it to him. I said, "Don't you ever lay that thing down again and walk off and leave it."

The Japs had planted mines all over the beach, but most of them were duds. They'd even buried bombs in the sand with the fuse end pointed up. We picked our way around them, but they took out some of our amtracs and DUKWs.

About thirty yards off the beach we found ourselves in what must have been a small coconut grove. Fire from both sides had shredded the trees and left a low forest of ragged stumps. Still, they gave us some kind of cover. You couldn't dig in the hard coral, but there were plenty of shell craters, and we hunkered down to catch our breath. Bullets were singing over our heads. The small Jap grenade launchers we called knee mortars were popping and artillery was rolling.

Our battalion had already lost its executive officer. Major Robert Ash was just stepping ashore when he was hit by artillery. The amtrac carrying our field telephones and communications personnel was burning out on the reef. We'd be without communications a good part of the day.

But K/3/5 had made it this far. Nobody in the mortar section had been hit.

Private First Class Eugene Sledge, one of my ammo carriers, was just behind me.

"Hey, Burgin," he said, "you got a cigarette?"

Sledge was a college kid who had given up officer training to become an enlisted man. I knew he was a nonsmoker.

"You're crazy, Sledgehammer," I said. "You don't smoke."

"I want a cigarette," he repeated.

I dug one out and handed it back to him.

A little bit later I looked around. He hadn't lit the thing. He was chewing on it. In fact, he had chewed it down to shreds.

———

The mortars and machine guns slacked off a bit and we got orders to move out.

We didn't know it at the time, but up on the north end of the beachhead, a thousand yards to our left, the First Marines' Third Battalion were getting the hell beat out of them. They'd landed on White Beach One with orders to take the high ground north of the airfield, and then got caught up in a bloody struggle for a foothold on a coral outcrop called the Point. Just south of them, Second Battalion had landed on White Beach Two. They were to link up with the Fifth Marines' First Battalion, which came ashore to their right, on Orange Beach One, with intentions to sweep across the airfield. As the Fifth Marines' Third Battalion, we'd be farther right, pushing across the south end of the field from Orange Beach Two. From the coconut grove we could see the south end of the runway a few dozen yards in front of us.

The Seventh Marines were supposed to land on our right, on Orange Beach Three. Their plan was to mop up resistance on the southeast corner of the island, then link up with us and swing north.

But the Seventh was already in trouble. Coming into shore, their Third Battalion ran into heavy fire from their right, and a number of their LVTs had to swing leftward and come in on our beach. Now there were two different Third Battalions where there should have been only one. To make it worse, both battalions had K companies.

For half an hour NCOs barked orders to find out who was who, trying to get things sorted out. The Seventh's K Company was shifted to our right, but now we were behind schedule. It would be another hour before we caught up with our own I Company, which was to our left. The morning's confusion would ripple through the rest of the day and by nightfall leave us in danger.

On the east side of the airfield, on the edge of a dense scrub forest, we came up on a Jap artillery piece firing away at the beach. They had a strange way of doing things. The six men working that gun were lined up, and as each took a turn firing it, that man would move off and the next man would step up, take his place, and fire. They just rotated around like ducks in a shooting gallery. We watched in amazement. Then we started shooting, picking them off one by one. As each one rotated around, we'd fire and he'd go down. Then the next one, and the next until there weren't any left. They never seemed to catch on.

Afterward, we dropped a grenade down the barrel of the gun. That seemed to finish it. Then we moved off into the forest. This was not the tropical jungle we'd fought through on New Britain. Peleliu was a thick tangle of stunted trees and vines that was the devil to get through but that screened our movements from the Japs who were up in the hills pounding everyone else. As we advanced we expected them to come screaming out of the trees in a banzai attack at any minute, like they had on New Britain. Instead we found only scattered snipers and bunkers. The bunkers weren't much more than piles of logs and rock, but they were impossible to see until you'd almost stepped on them. We had to knock out each one before we could move on.

Deep in the woods we came across the trail where we were supposed to turn north. Some of our riflemen pushed beyond and came out on the edge of a bay. The Seventh Marines, which were supposed to be on our right, were nowhere in sight.

Our riflemen shot some Japs who were thrashing across the mouth of the bay from one shore to the other. Then we were all ordered to head out and move north along the trail.

Peleliu has always been turned around in my mind. I never was able to get it straight, north and south, east and west, all the time we were on that island. I guess our sergeant, Johnny Marmet, may have had a map. The lieutenant had one. It turned out the maps were full of mistakes. They showed the mountains and the trees. They didn't show what was on the ground, or underneath it.

By early afternoon we lost contact with I Company on our left. A big gap opened up. L Company was moved forward with part of the Second Battalion that had been in reserve. But they couldn't find us. To tell the truth, we weren't sure where we were either. All we knew was that we were on a north-south trail somewhere in this scrub jungle.

We bumped into another nest of pillboxes and bunkers and had to wait for a tank to come forward and blast them out of our way.

By now communications had been reestablished. The Seventh Marines' Third Battalion—the same outfit that had got tangled up with us on Orange Beach Two—finally called in their position to headquarters. They were somewhere off to our right, on a trail. We had already reported we were on a trail running north through the scrub. We all assumed we were on the same trail, but they were a couple hundred yards ahead of us.

In fact they were south of us, where the trail branched and one part turned east.

Headquarters ordered their Third Battalion to stay put until we closed the gap. We started forward again. It was midafternoon. The heat was suffocating. We were dripping with sweat, sucking our canteens dry and popping salt tablets. We stumbled along expecting to encounter the Seventh Marines around the next bend in the trail. But by four p.m. we still hadn't run into them. We got further orders to keep moving until the scrub thinned out, east of the airfield.

We were all now stretched out like a rubber band. If a Jap counterattack hit us in the right spot, we'd snap.

We came out of the woods within full view of the airfield. On the far side, Jap artillery and mortar fire were building up to something, but we weren't their target. Most of their fire seemed to be landing to our left, back in the direction of Orange Beach Two, where the First and Second battalions had come ashore. A few shells sailed over our heads, landing somewhere behind us.

As we watched, a line of what we first thought were amtracs appeared from behind the hangars and barracks on the far side of the field and started rolling southwest, parallel to the main runway. Behind them we could see large groups of men moving forward. The firing picked up on both sides, and we realized we were watching Jap tanks and infantry. They had begun their expected counterattack.

We got orders to dig in and concentrate our fire on the infantry. Digging in the rock-hard coral was impossible, so we found craters and set up the mortars and began lobbing shells into the field.

The tank battle was no contest. Those little Jap tanks were thin-skinned and fragile, and our own Shermans, plus fire from bazookas and artillery, just tore the whole column apart in minutes. The foot soldiers melted away. We blinked and they were gone. Afterward, pieces of their tanks were scattered across the airfield like insect parts under a spiderweb.

But strung out along the edge of the scrub, we now had a fresh problem.

Sledge was holding a 60mm shell, just ready to drop it down the tube, when bullets started whining over our heads. They were coming from behind us. A stream of tracers passed over, close enough to dust his knuckles.

I turned in time to look down the barrel of a Sherman tank, its turret swiveling in our direction. He was parked in a clearing a hundred yards to our right. Beyond him came more tanks, and behind them, Marine riflemen, and they were shooting. Not past us, but *at* us!

Someone yelled at Sledge, and he froze. If a bullet hit that shell we'd all be blown to hell.

It was instantly clear to me what had happened. While we had been trying to catch up with the Seventh's Third Battalion in the woods, they had been behind us, waiting. Then they saw our mortar squad in front and assumed we were part of the Jap counterattack and opened fire. Those bright .50-caliber tracers that the Sherman tank was spitting would soon be followed by a 75mm shell from its cannon.

Everyone scrambled for cover. A shell crashed into the scrub just ahead of us.

I shouted, "Secure the mortars!" and took off toward the tanks, dodging from tree to tree and waving my arms. "Knock it off! Knock it off! You're gonna kill the whole damn bunch!"

Somehow over the racket I caught someone's attention and the firing died away.

In all the panic and confusion after the Seventh Marines had started firing at us, I did something that I'm not particularly proud of. Or I came very close to doing it.

One particular lieutenant had been making our lives miserable ever since we were on New Britain. Not that he was strict—he was worse.

He was two-faced. He'd lie and cover up. He'd order us to do something, then when someone higher up came down on him, he'd come down on us for doing what he'd told us to do in the first place. When he was needed, he could never be found. He had a way of disappearing when things got nasty. I'd already had one set-to with him that morning over a mortar emplacement.

When the Seventh Marines opened fire, I saw him do something no Marine should ever do: He turned and flat out ran. That yellow son of a bitch, I thought, running like that. I brought my M1 rifle up and got him in my sights. My finger was on the trigger. He vanished behind a log.

That yellow bastard, I thought. But I didn't shoot. Am I proud? Not particularly. If I had it to do over again, I wouldn't shoot him. It's a good thing I didn't.

———————————

It got dark pretty quickly. We still had no idea where I Company or L Company were situated, nor where we were supposed to be. Back at our battalion command post, behind the front lines, nobody knew where any of us were.

Sometime after the tank battle, a Jap mortar round had landed squarely on the post, spraying our commanding officer, Lieutenant Colonel Austin Shofner, with shrapnel and taking off the head of his communications officer, Captain R. F. Kehoe, Jr.

Shofner's wounds were serious enough to force his evacuation to a hospital ship. In the confusion word spread that he had been killed. He was almost a legend to us. He had been fighting on Corregidor when they surrendered to the Japs. They took him prisoner and he survived the Bataan Death March. After almost a year in a prison camp he organized a successful escape party and came back to the Marines to fight again.

Now, at the end of the first day of the invasion, Third Battalion's commanding officer lay wounded and out of commission. Our executive officer and communications officer were both dead. There was no longer any effective command. And we were scattered along a thin line through scrub jungle, out of touch with everyone else and surrounded by the enemy.

Our canteens were almost empty. We'd used up most of our ammunition. It was impossible to dig shelters, so we piled up rocks and logs and set up a perimeter defense. Machine guns rattled in the darkness and we fired off a few mortar rounds, more to make us feel good than to make the Japs feel bad.

From time to time a Navy destroyer lying offshore would fire a star shell. It would burst over our heads and come floating down on its parachute, shedding a yellowish glow over everything.

But it cast no light for us. Our luck had run out.

CHAPTER 1

A Marine's Story

They talk about the Greatest Generation. I've always thought the greatest generation that ever lived were my parents.

My dad, Joseph Harmon Burgin, was about six feet two. My mother, Beulah May Perry Burgin, was about five feet two. He could hold his arm straight out and she could walk under it and never touch it. I guess I took after my dad, but not quite as tall. I was only six one.

I was born in 1922, the third of seven children. I had two older sisters, three younger brothers and one younger sister.

My father had three younger brothers: George Burgin was the second child, and the twins, Remus and Romus. That's where I got my name, that and a four-year-old kid in our neighborhood named Valton Woods. Mother had never heard the name Valton, but she liked it. So, Romus Valton Burgin. There's not that many of us out there, I'll tell you.

All of us Burgin boys were in the military. Edgar and Bobby, my two youngest brothers, served in the Korean War. My other brother, Joseph Delton Burgin—we called him J.D.—was killed by artillery in Alsace-Lorraine on February 17, 1945. He had just got there.

I chose the Marines under circumstances I'll tell you about later.

In 1955 my mother and dad's farmhouse burned down, and all of our records, all my war souvenirs and everything else went with it. Nothing saved except a cedar chest and maybe a bed or two.

The farm was about eight miles from Jewett, Texas, which is seven miles southwest of Buffalo, almost halfway between Dallas and Houston. We were about three miles off Highway 79, running from Bryan to Palestine. My dad owned sixty acres, and then he had what we called "free range." I don't know who owned it. Most of it was timberland where we'd turn the cows out in the wintertime. In the summer and spring we'd keep them penned up in our pasture.

For the first six years, I went to a two-room schoolhouse, Friendship School. So did my two older sisters and one younger brother. When I finished the sixth grade in 1935, they consolidated the schools. After that we rode the bus into Jewett.

We had horses and mules, cultivators, middlebuster turning plows, planters. But no tractor. My father raised corn, cotton, sugarcane, and sorghum and we made sorghum syrup and ribbon cane syrup. But the cotton was his money crop. That was about the *only* money crop. I picked cotton from the time I was about three or four years old. My parents would give us a little sack, and we'd go along the rows and pick cotton. The one thing my mother and dad never did, they never did hold us out of school to help on the farm. But we would come in from school and change clothes and hit the field until dark. We helped Saturdays, Sundays and whenever we needed to get something done.

When we "lay by," as my dad called it—plowed for the last time, everything kind of waiting on the harvest—then he would take us down to Birch Creek and we'd fish. There wasn't anything in there but just little perch and little catfish. That was all it was. But it was a good outing.

My mother cooked three meals a day for nine people, and she worked in the field. The boys in the family, we did the housework just the same as the girls. My mother felt that if the girls can work in the fields, then the boys can do housework. So we all washed dishes, ironed, helped do washing—the whole nine yards.

She was a chef. She could make pies, cakes, soups. My wife, Florence, learned to make her soup with vegetables straight out of the garden. We still call it the Burgin Soup. Mother baked bread and made corn bread and biscuits. And we had milk cows, so we had milk to drink, and fresh butter.

She cooked everything on a woodstove. She washed in an old iron wash pot with a scrub board. She made most of our clothes. And she made her own soap, you know, make a pot of lye soap. She'd put up pickles and tomatoes in quart jars. She had a canner with a crank. You'd put a can in and fill it, and the canner would seal that rascal right up. We'd butcher a cow or a hog and she would can the meat.

We didn't have an icebox. We had a food cabinet with screen wires on the front and back so the air could circulate. We had a smokehouse built of logs with wooden shingles. My dad would go down on a little branch and find a tree that was pretty straight with no knots in it. He'd cut that down with an ax and crosscut saw, and saw it up in the lengths that he wanted for shingles. He had another tool with a big handle and a kind of ax-type blade on it, real sharp. He'd split the shingles to the thickness that he wanted. Then he would shingle that smokehouse that he had built out of logs.

Whenever we butchered one of the hogs and hung the hams and shoulders and the side that you make bacon out of in the smokehouse, it was my job before I started school to keep that fire burning. But not blazing, just let the smoke out of the hickory wood. I did that practically all day long. Dad would sugar-cure the meat, and it was absolutely delicious. No doubt about it.

We didn't have electricity and we didn't have indoor plumbing. When I was thirteen or fourteen we dug a well in our yard. I did most of the digging. My dad would pull the dirt up with a rope and a pulley in a deal that had a steel rim about two inches wide, about twelve to fourteen inches in diameter. A gunnysack made the bucket part. That way if it broke it wouldn't drop a metal bucket on me. At the end of the day he'd pull me out with the pulley.

We went down about thirty-two feet, and it was great water. The only trouble, if we had a drought it went dry. So we would have to haul the water from one of the branches and my mother would have to go down to the branch to wash her clothes. I would imagine it was pretty close to three-quarters of a mile.

We still didn't have electricity when I joined the Marine Corps in 1942. Rural Electrification finally came in sometime between 1942 and when I got home from the Marines in 1945.

———

I didn't want to miss a day of school. It wasn't because I wanted to learn. I just barely passed, I made Cs. But I liked being around other folks and playing whatever they were playing at the time. I didn't want to miss anything. I tell everybody that during my high school days I majored in PE and athletics. That's almost true. It didn't make any difference whether it was basketball, football, volleyball, track, or field. I was into it. I ran the low hurdles, high hurdles, pole vault, 440s. I was never a distance runner. I never ran a mile at one time in my whole life, even when I was in the Marines. But I was pretty speedy. I could run a fifty or a hundred in real good time.

I guess I liked football best. When I was a senior the team voted me captain. I still have the jacket with the star on it. I was always proud of that because the men voted me and not the coach. We weren't a .500 team, I'll tell you that. We won a few games, but not that many. But I enjoyed it. I would play basketball at night, but the bus wouldn't stay for the basketball players. After the ball game was over I'd walk eight miles home.

During Depression days there wasn't any money. There was a Works Progress Administration program in the schools, and they gave me the job of cleaning the gym. It paid three dollars a month. In the Depression a silver dollar—and silver dollars were plentiful in those days—looked as big as a wagon wheel. It was really something to get a silver dollar. Several dollars, man, that was something. That would carry me for a long time.

In the spring I picked berries and took them to town to sell for a dime a pail. Wild blackberries and dewberries. If we needed notebook paper or school supplies, mother would give me one or two dozen eggs and I'd take them in and sell them to merchants for a dime a dozen. You could take a dime and buy pretty much what you needed.

When I was about sixteen, Ed Hull, a neighbor, hired me for a couple or three days in the spring to chop cotton. There's a lot of grass and weeds that the plow won't get, and so you come in and chop cotton, that's what they call it. Thin down the stalks, cut the weeds out of it. I would be out there at the break of day and stay until it was dark. He fed me lunch and paid me seventy-five cents for the day. The next year he raised me to a dollar a day.

But farming wasn't one of my things. I'd seen my dad work hard only to see the crop fail. I thought, There's a better way to make a living than on the farm. I graduated from high school in May 1941, and as quick as I graduated I went to Dallas. My sister Ila was there and I lived with her until I found a place of my own.

My first job was in a warehouse for thirty cents an hour. I'll never forget that summer. We were unloading boxcars of candy bars. There were Snickers, Milky Ways, Baby Ruths, Butterfingers, all in eighty-pound boxes stacked chest high. The temperature was 110 to 115 a lot of days. The candy didn't melt, but *we* melted. We'd pull those boxes out of there and put them on a two-wheeler and roll them out and stack them in the warehouse—eighty pounds of those rascals. They were heavy. But I was young and I had played football, so it didn't bother me.

December 7, 1941, was a Sunday. I was at home listening to the radio when the news came over that the Japs had bombed Pearl Harbor. I don't think I really grasped the impact of what was happening. I knew a war had been brewing. Lots of folks had been gathering up iron and steel and selling it for about half a cent a pound. We knew where it was going—to Japan to make battleships. Even in high school we had joked about those guys shooting that steel back at us. But I didn't realize how Pearl Harbor would change the world, or how long we would be in it. Or how long *I* would be in it.

I went on working in the warehouse, but by February 1942 I was looking for another job. I read in the paper that a stationery company out of Columbus, Ohio, wanted a salesman to travel the country. I thought I'd go down and interview just to see what would happen. They hired me and put me on a sales crew.

We were driving brand-new 1941 Studebakers. The company provided two of them. Claude Malone was driving one of them. He was from Tennessee and I was with his crew. Then Bill Duebner, the owner, and his wife and another crew.

I loved it because I was getting an education that this old farm boy never knew. I had been to Houston and to San Antonio a few times and I'd been to Dallas half a dozen times. That was about as far off as I'd ever gone. I thought working for that stationery company was worth about two years of college, really, just being out in the world.

We started up through Oklahoma, went through Kansas, Nebraska, and Iowa, the Dakotas, Montana, Idaho, Washington State, Oregon, California. Then we came back through.

One day in the spring of 1942 we had just left Jamestown, North Dakota, heading for Bismarck. We came to a roadside diner and decided to stop for dinner. We were in the back end of the place washing up when two guys came in with guns drawn, one of them the local sheriff. They were looking for "those four guys that was in the Studebaker out there."

Well, that was us. The sheriff, who had a gimpy leg, deputized somebody right there on the scene, and they drove us in two cars back to Jamestown. Then they locked us up for the night.

I'd been in a jail. When I was in sixth grade, going to that two-room schoolhouse near Jewett, our teacher took a carload of us boys to visit the state penitentiary in Huntsville. I can still hear, walking those aisles with the cells on either side of you, those guys hollering at us, the guards clanging those big steel doors.

On the way home, the teacher said to us, "Boys, you don't ever want to be in there. You don't ever want to go to jail."

And now here I was in jail. For what, I couldn't even begin to imagine.

We didn't get anything to eat that night. The next morning they brought us cold oatmeal.

We'd ask the jailer whenever he came by, "What's going on? What's happening here?"

"You'll find out soon enough."

About four o'clock that afternoon they came and let us out. The sheriff's wife had made fresh rolls for us, with butter.

We sat there eating them, gratefully.

"Well," I finally said, "this is the first time I've been in jail. Just for the record, what the hell were we in for?"

"First off," the sheriff said, "you was driving a brand-new Studebaker. And we thought that might not be right. So we were checking for a stolen car.

"And then we thought, that car is registered in Ohio, and you're up here in North Dakota. So we thought you might be draft dodgers. So it just took time to get all the information that you was okay."

"Okay," I said. "That's all I wanted to know."

I was twenty, not yet of draft age. But the war had already thrown its shadow across my path.

My story is the story of hundreds of thousands who fought for our country in World War II. In a way, there's nothing special about it. In another way, everyone who fights for his or her country has a special story to tell.

In 2004 and 2006 I was asked to present the Old Breed Award for distinguished service in the First Marine Division. At these gatherings there are always five or six World War II vets. The young guys, young Marines, always gather around to hear our stories.

One of them, a mortarman, asked me, "They don't shoot mortarmen, do they? I mean, you're always behind the lines."

"Let me tell you something," I said. "They don't discriminate. They shoot *anybody*. I lost several men to rifle fire. A firefight is a firefight, whether it's in the South Pacific or Korea or Vietnam or Iraq or Afghanistan."

But I understood what he meant.

I have a photograph on my wall at home. There we all are, what's left of K Company, on the beach at Peleliu. We're waiting for the ship to take us somewhere, anywhere away from the battle. That young mortarman could be any one of us.

I look at that picture today and I think, I don't remember I was ever that young.

CHAPTER 2

Mortarman

I'd made up my mind that when the draft caught up with me I was going into the Air Force or the Navy or the Marines. Anything but the Army.

I was a year out of high school and the war was on. I'd been on the road with the crew, selling personalized engraved stationery from the company based in Columbus, Ohio. Everywhere we went I saw the Marine recruiting posters in front of post offices. They didn't show them in their greens. They always had them in dress blues. I thought the Marines looked like a sharp outfit. Disciplined. Elite. I was from a farm. I was used to hard work and discipline. The Army seemed sloppy to me.

Sometimes folks on the road would ask why I wasn't in the service. The truth was, I wasn't of draft age. But that was complicated to explain.

So I told them, "I'm going to join the Marines next Friday." It was always next Friday, no matter what day or week it was. And always the Marines.

When the draft finally did catch me, in September of 1942, our crew was in Kentucky. The notice had arrived several weeks before at my parents' farm near Jewett. I was ordered to report to the local draft board over in Centerville, the Leon County seat. By now there was no time. So I went to the closest draft board I could find, in Catlettsburg, Kentucky, and explained my situation. They said they couldn't process me. I pointed out that it was all the same military and the same U.S. government. Why couldn't they process me and send the papers to my local draft board?

We argued for what seemed like the better part of the day. Finally they gave in and examined me and promised to forward the papers to Centerville. After that I quit selling and went home to the farm and waited. The next notice I got was that I was being drafted into the Army. I was to report November 12 to Centerville.

Instead I went down to Houston on the tenth and bunked overnight with a buddy. The next day the Air Force told me there was a six-week waiting list. The Navy recruiter was a smart aleck. So I walked across the street to the Marine Corps office. They examined me, poked and prodded, and then filled out the forms. But I wasn't twenty-one yet, and the recruiting sergeant told me I needed written permission from a parent or guardian before I could enlist. I figured I was either in the Marines or I was in trouble with the draft board.

That afternoon the recruiter sent a telegram to my father up on the farm. I spent another night with my friend, then got to the recruiting station the next morning just as the recruiter was turning the key in the lock. We stepped inside together. During the night someone had poked a telegram under the door. It was from Papa: Permission granted.

The Marines fed me breakfast and put me on a train to San Antonio. I may have slept on the train that night; I don't remember. But I do remember that the next morning, November 13, I was sworn in along with dozens of others, mostly kids like myself from hardscrabble farms and small towns all over south Texas. They fed us breakfast and then put us on another train and shipped us west.

_____

Our second day out, somewhere beyond El Paso, we got our first taste of life in the United States Marine Corps.

We were in New Mexico or Arizona, I figured, rolling through the desert toward California. The whole train was full of recruits. So were dozens of other trains that day, carrying young guys like me to training camps, bases and ports. The railroaders called them "main trains," because they had priority over everything else on the track.

There were sixty or so of us in our coach, mostly dozing or staring out the windows. We were still wearing our civilian clothes except for one Marine in uniform. He was sitting three seats back from me and across the aisle, and his armband identified him as an MP. A younger man in street clothes was sitting beside him. I assumed he must be some kind of prisoner, because he was doing his best to give the MP a hard time. His mouth had been going since San Antonio. And he was a jitterbug. Every few minutes, it seemed he had to go to the restroom. He'd jump up and the MP would march him to the end of the coach and wait in the aisle while he finished his business, whatever he was doing in there. Then they'd come back down the aisle to their seats. The fellow would flop down and pretty soon his mouth would be running again. If it wasn't the restroom it was a drink of water or a smoke or some other thing. He had the whole car on edge.

Finally he stood and said something—I didn't catch what—that pushed the MP over the edge.

"I want you to sit down, shut up and don't be aggravating me anymore," the MP snapped. "If you don't sit down and shut up, I'm going to knock the hell out of you."

The prisoner kept yacking and the MP got up, billy club in hand. There was a loud *crack!* and the guy went down with a couple bloody teeth in his lap. For the rest of the trip he sat bleeding into a handkerchief. But he didn't say a thing.

The rest of that day word went up and down that coach among the recruits: "Yeah, you don't argue with authority."

Sometime around eight or nine o'clock the second night out the train pulled into boot camp. We were ordered out of the cars and told to stand with our toes touching a white line on the pavement and with our bags on our right. Then they read out our names and marched us to the barracks.

We couldn't see a thing in the darkness. That's the way they always tried to do it with recruits, bring you in at night. You're disoriented, you can't get your bearings, you don't know what's coming. They're in charge.

I was apprehensive, but I wasn't scared. I didn't think they could dish out anything that I couldn't handle.

Bunks were double stacked along both walls. Beside each bunk was a wooden chest, which we learned was our locker, and a galvanized pail. We'd find out what the pail was for the next morning. We were in our bunks before midnight. It seemed like I had just closed my eyes when they sounded reveille, right inside the door. And it was loud. The drill instructor was hollering, "Hit the deck, you bunch of sorry punks."

And we did hit the decks. Guys were banging on the floor, metal bunks were rattling. For the next six weeks those were the sounds that started off every day, our alarm clock: reveille and clanging bunks and the DI shouting at us "punks." We were never Marines. We were the sorriest bunch of human beings they'd ever set eyes on.

It must have been six a.m., still dark outside. I thought, What the hell have I got myself into?

We marched to the chow line and got breakfast. Then we were ordered to pick up our pails and follow the sergeant. Next everybody lined up for a haircut. In those days long hair was not the style, even if you weren't in the Marines. But one kid did wear his hair curled and hanging down, like he was proud of it. The barber asked him, "Do you want to keep these curls?"

"Yes, sir, I sure do."

"Okay," the barber said. With his clippers he sheared up one side of that kid's head and down the other. Then he handed the kid his locks. "Here, keep these."

After haircuts, we went to the supply room, pails in hand, to draw our clothes—socks, shoes, underwear, dungarees. The recruits who had already been through the line were yelling at us, "You'll be sorry." The guys behind the counter handing out the clothes were giving us a hard time, too. You had to wear what they gave you. You didn't go back and exchange it. There were only two sizes in the Marine Corps: too big and too damned big.

They did ask what size shoe you wore, so your shoes always fit good for marching. They were high-tops, maybe ankle length. The smooth side of the leather was on the inside, the rough side out. And every cotton-picking day you had to shine those shoes so the DI could see his face in them. By the end of boot camp, you had them gleaming like a new car. The brown polish came in a little tin they issued along with the clothes, shaving gear, toothpaste and toothbrush, and a bar of soap. It all went into the pail. We had to buy a copy of the little red book, the *Marine's Handbook*, for $1. The 242-page "Seventh Edition." Over the weeks ahead we'd just about memorize it. I think they took $10 out of our first month's pay for the whole bucketful of goodies.

They told us to strip out of our street clothes, put them in a cardboard box, and write our home address on the outside of the box. That was the last we'd see of our street clothes. Then, with pails in hand, Marine uniforms over our left arms, shoes strung around our necks by their laces, they marched us buck naked back to the barracks. Here they gave us padlocks for our lockers. We drew two sheets, two Marine blankets and a pillowcase each. And we got our dog tags. There was a pair of them on the string, one hanging from the other. They were still brass in those days. Later they went to aluminum. Each was stamped with our name and military identification number. Mine was 496798. We were told the dog tags must remain around our necks at all times. They didn't tell us then that if we died in combat, one of the dog tags would be sent to an office in Washington as a record of our death. The other would stay with our body and eventually hang from the cross over our grave.

We signed all sorts of papers, took some tests, got our shots.

We learned that Marines had their own name for everything. The floors were the deck. The walls were bulkheads, the ceiling was the overhead, stairs were ladders. The bathroom was the head, and was to be kept spotless at all times. We were not to leave the barracks unless we had permission. We were taught how to make up the bunks and how to stow our gear in the lockers. You had to get down on your hands and knees to open them because the key was on the same string as your dog tags, and we were forbidden to take that string off. There was a place for everything and everything had to be in its place.

Two corporals took charge of sixty of us. They were our DIs, and they were to be obeyed. When one of them entered the squad room, whoever saw him first yelled "Attention!" and we all snapped to.

Our rifles were issued a few days later. The M1903 Springfield weighed eight pounds and eleven ounces. We did physical drill every day, and we'd stand holding that heavy rifle at arm's length, shoulder high—and hold it and hold it. When they got through with us, our arms were so tired that the rifle felt like it weighed eighty pounds.

We drilled with them, but we didn't fire them yet.

One of the few times I got in trouble was over my rifle. During rifle inspection, you hold the weapon up and the DI grabs it and inspects it. I guess.

I hung on to mine a little too tight. At least that's what he thought.

"Oh, you love that rifle, do you?" he said.

I said, "Yes, sir!"

Our DIs were corporals, but it was always "Yes, sir!" and "No, sir!"

"Okay, you can sleep with it tonight," he said. "You put that right in your bunk when you go to bed and you take it out when you get up in the morning. You sleep with that rifle tonight if you like it so well."

"Yes, sir!"

Sure enough, sometime during the night—I don't know exactly what time it was—he came around to check if that rifle was in the bunk with me. And it was there, right beside me.

We "dry fired" the rifle for days, practicing the same sequence over and over—align the sight, adjust for wind and distance, breath control, gentle trigger squeeze, follow-through—before we got to shoot live ammunition. On the range some of the guys couldn't get their arm positioned where the instructor wanted it. When you're shooting they want that arm squarely under that rifle, straight up and down. Some guys were just not flexible. They couldn't bring their arm over that far. They had a helluva time. So the DI would take their arm and yank it— *uh!*—and finally get it where it belonged.

There were three rankings, from Marksman to Sharpshooter up to Expert: I shot Sharpshooter with the .45 pistol and Springfield.

They worked us day and night. They'd come into the barracks at eleven o'clock at night. You hadn't been in bed maybe an hour, and they'd shout, "We're moving out! We're shipping overseas. Get it all together." We had to get our seabag, our full transport pack, our shelter half, the whole nine yards. We'd hit the streets and they'd march us for an hour and a half. Then we'd come back and get a little sleep and maybe at three o'clock they'd get us up again. We did a lot of running in the sand, and if you weren't in pretty good shape that was tough. Your foot was slipping back every time it hit the sand. It was like trying to run in one of those dreams where your feet move but you don't get anywhere.

Our DIs were named Stallings and Simon. Stallings stood about five feet eleven and straight as an arrow. He was an athletic type, and you knew not to mess with him.

Simon was soft-spoken and wore dark glasses. I had a little trouble with him one time in the chow line. When you're in the chow line you're at ease. You can move around but you can't talk.

Fighter planes were buzzing off the runway on North Island, sometimes two at a time and flying real low. I was standing there stargazing at those airplanes, and I said, half to myself, "My God, watch them go!"

Simon walked up to me and stuck his face right up in mine. "You are at ease. Do you understand that?"

Whenever he had something to say to you, Simon got right up in your face and looked you straight in the eye and spoke very softly. I doubt if the third man down the line heard what he said. But *you* heard what he said. And you knew he meant business.

I thought then, That's a good tactic. You don't need to yell and scream at somebody to get something done. Later on I was to make good use of that lesson.

We had school and if anybody dozed off during class, it was so many laps around the parade ground.

Whenever the sleeper would get back, the DI would say, "Are you tired?"

"No, sir!"

"Well, go again."

He'd come back with his tongue hanging, absolutely give out. And the DI would say, "Are you tired now?"

"A little bit, sir!"

"Do you think you can stay awake, now?"

"Yes, sir!"

We had two sets of fatigues, and whenever we quit for the day we went to the laundry, where there were scrub benches, brushes and soap. We washed the clothes we had worn that day, and put on the fresh set.

One kid thought he could get away with something. He would just wet one set of clothes and hang them out to dry and wear the old set again. The DI caught him and made him strip down to his underwear. Then he lined up the whole platoon in formation out in the street. He took both sets of that guy's clothes, soaked them, and laid them in the sand and marched us down and about-face and back over those clothes maybe ten times. Then he made the kid go wash them.

Another morning, a guy didn't shave. Or maybe he shaved, but it wasn't a close shave. His jaw bristled. The DI got up in his face. "Oh, you forgot to shave this morning."

He said, "No, sir. I shaved but my face was sore and I didn't do too good a job."

"I don't think you did, either," the DI said. "Come down and see me this afternoon whenever we get through."

That afternoon he went in and the DI was sitting there whittling on a piece of wood with a razor blade. He snapped that blade in the razor and tightened it down. Then he said, "Crawl under that bunk." He handed him the razor and he made him dry shave lying on the floor beneath that bunk.

No doubt about it. They had ways to get our attention. They broke us down. They didn't only train us physically. They trained us mentally. Boot camp was normally a twelve-week course. They put us through it in six weeks. We were an experiment. They worked us, as this younger generation likes to say, 24-7.

When I went into the Marines, I never thought about killing anybody. By the time that six weeks was up I was lean and I was mean. I can honestly say I could have cut a Jap's throat and never blinked an eye.

_____

When we graduated from boot camp we were given the Marine Corps Globe and Anchor to wear on our collars. Only after that did they finally call us Marines. Later classes got a week's leave to go home and show off to the folks after graduation, but we never got a leave, and my folks never got to see me in uniform. Instead we were trucked twenty or thirty miles over to Camp Elliott, an old Navy base the Marines were using for advanced training. We were assigned to the Ninth Replacement Brigade. The first day or so someone came along and told me, "You're going to be in the sixty mortars. Report to that tent over there."

The mortar. I didn't even know there was such a weapon. That first day they had it set up behind a tent, and we all got acquainted.

The M2 60mm mortar—the 60—is a deadly weapon. One mortar shell can pretty much be depended on to kill everyone within a forty-five-foot radius. It's a little slower than an artillery shell, but it's reliable and very effective. The biggest battlefield killer is not the rifle, and not artillery. It's the mortar. If you're firing artillery, you fire straight to the target, and it hits at a low angle. But you can fire a mortar at a high angle and it comes almost straight down. It can get into places that artillery and rifle fire can't. A man can't hide from a mortar. They said that on Guadalcanal a gunnery sergeant named Lou Diamond put one right down the smokestack of a Japanese ship.

Our classroom was in an open pavilion about thirty feet long, with a metal roof and rows of picnic tables. They had set up a mortar just outside, and the instructor started by giving us the breakdown on the weapon: the base plate, the firing tube, the bipod, the M4 sight, and the rounds themselves. We learned there were six men in a mortar squad—

three ammo carriers, a gunner, assistant gunner and the squad leader, who is usually a corporal. In battle the gunner carries the base plate, which weighs about twelve pounds. His assistant carries the tube, which is eight or ten pounds. The squad leader carries the sight, which has a level indicator and is marked for degrees right and left.

A 60mm round weighs three pounds. Around the base of the round there are four firing charges, or increments, tabs of propellant about the size of postage stamps and maybe an eighth of an inch thick. You leave the increments on or pull them off depending on how far you want to fire the round. If your target is, say, fifteen hundred yards away, you leave all four of them on. If it's fifty yards, you take off all but one.

They call mortars "hip pocket artillery." The whole deal—base, bipod, tube and sight—sets up in seconds. The most complicated thing is getting the round on target. When you're dug in, you set an aiming stake out in front of the mortar and zero in the sight on that. The squad leader is probably twenty-five or thirty yards ahead, on the front lines with the riflemen. He's wired in to the gunner by what we called a sound-powered phone. He calls in the range to the target, number of degrees right or left of the aiming stake, and gives the commands to fire. The gunner makes adjustments on the tube and his assistant drops in the round. The kill radius is about forty-five feet.

At Camp Elliott they trained us and trained us. I got to where I could set up the mortar in my sleep. But I didn't get to fire the 60 but once or twice all the time I was in the States. I began to wonder if we would ever get to put this skill to use.

———————

The Marines never gave you advance warning when they were about to send you someplace. You were the last to know. One morning at Camp Elliott we got word, "Fall out. We're shipping out." For all we knew, it might have been another drill, but this time it wasn't. We rode trucks down to the San Diego docks and climbed aboard the USS *Mount Vernon*.

The next day, March 12, 1943, we sailed.

The ship stopped off in Honolulu, Fiji, and New Caledonia, but we never went ashore. I figured they were pulling in for supplies or more troops. It was an uneventful trip. For lack of anything better to do, we spent a lot of time just standing on deck trading rumors. At Fiji I looked over the side and watched dark hammerhead sharks swarming around the ship. I got to be pretty good friends with another Marine, Jim Burke. He was from Clinton, Iowa, where his brother owned a bar.

On the last day of March, we pulled into Port Melbourne, Australia.

We were trucked forty miles southeast of the city to Camp Balcombe. It was a pretty place with green fields and gentle hills that reminded me of Texas. The camp was full of Marines from the First Division's Fifth Regiment, resting up and retraining after the Battle of

Guadalcanal. We were just raw recruits from the Ninth Replacement Battalion, the newcomers. They put us in with the veterans. In the months ahead they became our teachers.

For the first week or so we didn't do much. We were assigned to occasional work parties, policing the grounds, picking up trash, dumping the garbage, doing whatever needed to be done. Then I was sent to the Fifth Regiment Headquarters and Service Company, where I was put on KP. Not as punishment for anything I'd done, but just to keep me busy and because somebody had to do the work.

One of the sights around camp was Lou Diamond, the legendary 60mm sharpshooter and one of the Marines' Old Breed. He had fought in World War I and after that at Shanghai and finally at Guadalcanal. Now he was assigned as sergeant of the guard at the brig while awaiting shipment home because he was too old to fight. He wore a little goatee and the word was he drank Australian beer by the case.

Diamond had an old cat, and every morning you'd hear that foghorn voice of his calling, "Come on, Tom. Come on, Tom." That cat would follow him everywhere, all day, like a dog.

After I'd been on KP for about three months, they pulled me out and said, "You're going up to Third Battalion, K Company. Mortars."

It was my specialty, but in the Marines you never know where they'll put you. You just wait.

I moved a couple hundred yards from headquarters. The barracks was large enough to hold both the machine gun and mortar sections. Jim Burke was there.

They began to train us constantly. At the rifle range, I shot poorly with the BAR—Browning Automatic Rifle—but finally shot Expert with the M1, which was just being issued. Shortly after that I was promoted to private first class.

We marched. We would head out in the mornings, early, head up the road twenty miles and get back in the afternoons, late, carrying a full pack and our weapons.

One day we had a competition to detail strip a machine gun, an M1, and mortar, see who could tear it down and put it back together the fastest. I could put that mortar together and get it on target faster than anybody. I mean, I was the head dog. I made gunner immediately and was issued a .45, which I wore from then on.

I think that competition was when I was first noticed. I was a gunner on New Britain. On Peleliu I was a corporal, an observer and squad leader. By Okinawa I would be sergeant in charge of the mortar section.

———————

The Australians had been in the war longer than we had. They sent their Diggers—as they called soldiers—to fight the Germans in 1940 when I was still picking cotton and playing high school football. The day before the Japanese bombed us at Pearl Harbor, Australian airplanes fired on a Jap convoy off the coast of Malaya. Two months later, Japanese planes bombed Darwin on Australia's northern coast. In March 1943, they were expecting a Jap invasion at any time.

Even at Melbourne, on the southern coast, the war seemed pretty close. U.S. Marines were everywhere—the First Marine Division had taken over the new Royal Melbourne Hospital for the wounded and malaria cases from Guadalcanal. The division's First Marine Regiment was quartered on the city's cricket grounds, and the Seventh Marines were out at Mount Martha, right up the hill from Camp Balcombe. On weekends and leave days we poured into the city to enjoy the beautiful parks and broad streets, the bars and sweetshops. And to tell the truth, the girls, who were at least as pretty as American girls.

Once I was assigned to KP duty I lost no time working out a deal with the mess sergeant. I would work a straight twenty-four hours, then get twenty-four hours off to go into town. As soon as I was free, I'd shower, put on a fresh uniform, find Jim Burke, and we'd head out.

We'd catch what we called the cattle car, an eighteen-wheeler with a trailer that had board benches along the sides and down the middle. You could sit on that or straddle it—neither was comfortable—for the ride to Frankston, where we'd catch the train into Melbourne.

The city had streetcars and buses, the first double-decker buses I ever saw. Trains left for the suburbs every three or four minutes. You could go anywhere and you didn't have to wait all day to do it.

We'd pull into the big Flinders Street Station about ten a.m. Jim usually spent the day across the street in the bar at the Young & Jackson Hotel, where the big attraction, other than strong beer, was *Chloe*, a very big and very pink painting of a naked young lady. Every GI in Melbourne had to pay his respects to *Chloe* at least once.

I might have a couple beers with Jim, but then I would go sightseeing. But first we would have some business to attend to.

Jim had requested that the Marines send his allotment home to Clinton so his folks could bank it for him. But for some reason, the Corps went on paying him full salary, too. By the time someone caught the mix-up, he owed the Marines a lot of money. So they cut him to $5 a payday until it was paid off. That wasn't enough to go on liberty.

Before we went out on the town, Jim and I would go to the PX and each buy three cartons of cigarettes at fifty cents per carton. We were getting good American brands—Lucky Strikes, Camels and Chesterfields—not those wartime cigarettes like Fleetwoods. We'd hide them in the short wool jackets they'd issued us—Eisenhower jackets—take them into Melbourne and walk down the street until we sold them. We were getting two and a half Australian pounds a carton, and the exchange rate was about two and a half American dollars on the pound. You could buy a pint of beer for about twelve cents. Steak and eggs cost fifty cents. About thirty cents would get you into a movie. So six cartons would get Jim through liberty that weekend.

Late one Sunday afternoon in April, Jim and I were walking down Collins Street when we found ourselves following two young women, a blonde and a brunette, both very pretty. When they stepped into a milk bar—a combination sweetshop and soda fountain very popular in Melbourne—Jim and I stopped and looked at each other.

"The brunette's mine," I said.

"I'll take the blonde," he said.

We stepped inside, where the salesgirl was just weighing the candy the girls bought. "I'll wait on you next," she said.

"Never mind," Jim said, nodding at the two girls. "We're with them."

"I'll have what she's having," I said, indicating the brunette.

Outside the shop we asked their names. The brunette was Florence Riseley and her friend was Doris Moran. They said they were eighteen. They had come downtown from Albert Park, a suburb, to meet Florence's mother and three-year-old brother, who were from Tasmania and would be taking a train that evening. Since none of us had anything to do for a couple hours, the girls offered to show us the Melbo Museum, which was a few blocks away.

The museum's main attraction turned out to be a stuffed racehorse named Phar Lap, which Doris informed us had been poisoned by "you Yanks" while racing in the United States. After about thirty minutes in the museum, staring at exhibits, Jim complained that everything in the place was starting to smell as dead as the horse.

"We told you that you Yanks killed him," the girls said and laughed.

We walked them back to Flinders Street Station, where Florence's mother and little brother had already arrived and were waiting to catch a local to the suburbs in an hour.

While Florence and her mother talked, Jim and I took turns entertaining her brother with train sounds and piggyback rides up and down the platform. It was the right move.

"They seem to be nice," Florence's mother whispered to her daughter. "Anybody who plays with a child like that can't be all bad."

When it came time to go and we said our good-byes, Florence's mother slipped her a twenty-pound note. "I was wondering where we were going to eat," Jim muttered to me. Florence heard him.

We found another milk bar nearby and the four of us had a pretty good meal by Australian standards—meat pies and milk shakes. When the waitress brought the bill, Jim and I pointed to Florence.

"It's hers," we said.

we got up to go I saw Florence's eyes flash and her jaw tighten. Just as we got to the cash register, I slipped the bill out of her hand and, as I'd planned all along, paid it myself. We all had a good laugh over that.

The evening was young. The train back to Frankston didn't leave until 11:55 and the girls' train to the suburbs left at midnight. So we took a boat ride on the Yarra River. If you get a bunch of Australians together, no matter where, pretty soon they'll start to sing. So we drifted down the Yarra River, passengers singing "A Boy in Khaki" and "Bye for Now," and, of course, "Waltzing Matilda."

At the station, they gave us big hugs, and we agreed to meet the following Saturday at seven p.m. under the station clocks. At six minutes to midnight, Jim and I climbed aboard the train to Frankston, which started rolling almost as soon as we took our seats. Through the window we could see Florence and Doris take off on a dead run. Their train was several platforms over and it left in just five minutes. I noticed Florence had long legs.

Almost every Saturday for the next three months, Jim and I would meet Florence and Doris at Flinders Street. We'd ride around in one of the city's horse-drawn buggies, cracking American jokes, which the girls seemed to enjoy. Sometimes, we'd pay six pence and walk downstairs to a movie house where they showed continuous newsreels of the war, or we'd go out to Luna Park, an amusement park by the river.

Florence and I spent a lot of time just sitting on benches in the city's gardens—Melbourne had some of the most beautiful flower gardens in the world—talking about our families, about what was going on in the world and about life before the war. And after. She was easy to talk with.

I found out her father operated a steam shovel in the coal mines at Yollourn North, about ninety miles from Melbourne, and that he had fought in France during World War I, where he had been gassed. I also found out that she was sixteen, not eighteen. She had lied about her age to get a job at a factory making biscuits for the troops. Her boss had been so impressed by her work that he made her assistant floor supervisor over twenty-four other girls, and the company was sending her to night school to study management. So I knew she was smart.

One weekend I rode the train with her to Albert Park, where she lived with her uncle. At her front yard, she stepped inside the gate and swung it closed between us. Then she leaned forward and gave me my first kiss.

We've laughed about that over the years—that she had to put the gate between us.

On August 13, my birthday, Jim and I met the girls, and since it was a special day, we had some drinks. Then we all went to the Tivoli Theatre, where they had beautiful dancing girls wearing big feathers and not much else. The show was almost sold out, but we got tickets for the third balcony. I remember stumbling up the stairs, Florence in front of me, counting steps and trying to remember if we had passed the second balcony. I also remember we finished the evening in a movie theater, where Florence held my dizzy head in her lap and gently kissed me.

———————————

Something was in the wind. They were picking up the pace of training over the whole division. We started pulling field exercises with the Guadalcanal vets, crawling under barbed wire with our rifles, live ammunition zinging a few feet over our heads. We'd run, hit the deck, get up and run again. We'd practice making landings in rubber boats, all of it as if the enemy were right in front of us. The Guadalcanal vets had already been through it with real Japs. Just hanging around the barracks listening to those guys was an education. They'd tell stories about how they nearly starved to death on Guadalcanal, how they came down with malaria or dysentery, how they had to fight the Japs stationed on the island and then had to fight the reinforcements the Japs brought in. Just good talk between fighting men.

More than anything, we learned about tactics, both ours and the enemy's. Of course, they'd taught us all that in boot camp and at Camp Elliott—we knew enough that when someone called out "Hit the deck!" we shouldn't stand there asking questions. But the men from Guadalcanal were an advanced course. They'd been there and they'd done it.

Jap snipers would tie themselves in the treetops. You couldn't see them, but they were there, watching and waiting. They'd cut fire lanes through the trees, narrow breaks about three or four feet wide at right angles to our line of march. They'd set up a machine gun and when a line of Marines would come along they'd open fire. You'd be like pins in a bowling alley.

Or you'd be moving along a trail, single file, and a Jap would get in behind the last man in the column and bayonet him or slit his throat. You'd never hear him go down. Then they'd get the next man, and the next, picking them off one by one.

I sat and listened whenever they were telling war stories, and I'd ask questions. What happened, when did it happen, how did it happen? I paid attention because I knew that we were soon going into the same situation, or something as bad.

They canceled all leaves, and we could no longer go into the city. I wrote Florence a long letter: "We are pretty busy getting ready for you know what. But from what I can find out we are going to be here for another 3 to 6 weeks. . . . We are making rubber boat landings up until Friday, I know, but I don't know what is beyond that."

We'd been at Camp Balcombe five months. One evening they told us to get our gear together. We were moving out.

We marched out of camp about dusk and hiked all that night. We'd walk for fifty minutes and break for ten, walk fifty minutes and break for ten. In the morning, field cooks met us and had breakfast ready. Then we took off again and hiked all day, fifty and ten all the way. That night we stopped and ate again. Me and Jim Burke figured we were going to spend the night, so we pitched our pup tent. About the time we got it up, someone yelled "Fall in!"

You never saw two Marines tear down a pup tent and get back in formation so fast in your life.

We had a pace we had to maintain, and we wore our full transport packs, upper and lower part, with a bedroll. The whole thing weighed about forty pounds. We were carrying our M1s and I had that .45 strapped to my side and was carrying the butt plate for the mortar. Whenever they hollered "break," I'd just lean back on that pack and instantly I was gone. I must have slept nine minutes out of every ten-minute break.

We hiked all that second night, and starting the next morning we pulled maneuvers all day long. Sherman tanks, artillery, machine guns, all firing live ammunition, aircraft bombing and strafing out ahead of us. We'd be crawling along on our bellies and they were firing right over our heads. You'd hear the bullets zinging. It was as near combat as you could get.

About four o'clock in the afternoon we started hiking back. Somewhere along the way, they sent trucks out to pick us up, and what a blessing that was. It was Friday afternoon. We'd been at it since Wednesday. And as tired as everyone was, we still went into town on Saturday.

By now Florence and I had most of six months together. I don't know that there was one moment when I could have said that we were in love. It was just a slow process in which we began to care for each other. We talked about me going into the war. We knew that it was going to happen sooner or later. We didn't know when.

Toward the end of September they took our dress uniforms, our greens and hats and shoes. We went on liberty wearing our khakis and combat boots. We called them "boondockers." Florence hadn't even been expecting me. I looked all over town for her and finally found her with a bunch of her girlfriends in St. Kilda Park, where we had sat and talked so often.

She knew the minute she saw me.

We just hung on to each other. I kept saying, "I'll be all right. I'll be all right."

I would have loved to have married her right then. But I had sense enough to know what was ahead of me. I didn't have a clue how long it would last. I knew I couldn't even think about marrying her and going off and getting killed and leaving her a widow.

"I'll be all right," I said. "I'll come back for you when it's over."

But I was wrong.

CHAPTER 3

Green Hell

The Sunday morning after Florence and I said our good-byes, they rousted us out of bed at six and told us to get our gear together. The First and Second battalions had already shipped out by the end of August. Shortly afterward the Seventh Marines had moved to the docks. We knew we were next.

After breakfast we were trucked down to Port Melbourne. We stood around all morning before finally climbing the ramp to the *B. F. Shaw*, a Liberty Ship.

Then we waited some more.

All that day and into the night we stood along the rails and watched the *Shaw* take on cargo. Little by little the mountains of crates piled all over the dock, the rows of trucks and jeeps, the artillery and deflated rafts and stacks of stretchers were lifted and lowered into the hold. I didn't know a ship could carry so much. They had loading down to a science. The least important stuff went in first, then the more important, and finally whatever would be needed right away, like ammunition and drums of fuel. Last on, first off.

That ship sure wasn't designed to carry troops. We were stuffed into the cargo hold with our gear. We'd sleep in hammocks stacked four and five high and slung between riveted bulkheads and columns. Make-do plumbing facilities were up on the open deck. The chow lines were slow and stretched for yards.

We steamed out of Port Phillip Bay into the ocean the next morning, September 27, then swung around to the north. We had only a general idea where we were headed—to some island someplace. To the war.

We sailed on for a little over a week without incident before pulling in one afternoon at Goodenough Island off the eastern coast of New Guinea. The Australians had cleaned the Japs out the year before, and the First Battalion had already set up an advance camp. We were able to disembark and walk around for a couple hours and get our land legs back. After the gentle, rolling country around Melbourne, Goodenough was a change in scenery and a glimpse of things to come. There was a coastal strip of jungle, then a steep, rugged slope leading up to a sharp volcanic peak. That night we were back aboard ship when a Jap plane came over, low. You couldn't see him but you could hear him. He dropped a bomb without hitting anything and flew off. But he let us know we were in the war zone.

The next morning we pulled out and three days later, on October 11, we landed at Milne Bay, New Guinea. That would be our home for almost three months. The letters Florence had been writing in Melbourne—the first of hundreds—finally caught up with me. And I wrote my first letters to her.

We found a camp scraped out of the jungle. Rows of tents were set up on either side of a sort of road bulldozed through the mud. The rains came and went, and came and went again. The tents were wet, the ground was wet, our clothes were wet. When we went to lie down, our cots would sink into the muck so that we soon found ourselves sleeping on the ground with only a layer of canvas beneath us. Mornings we stood in formation, ankle-deep in the muddy "street." Between rains we dried out a little. They scattered some crushed rock around, and that helped a bit.

Mud or not, we still observed the old Marine tradition of cleanliness. Company headquarters was down at the end of the street, and right behind that was a little branch creek. It became our laundry. We'd take a bar of Marine soap and a scrub brush and go down there and find a rock, maybe about a foot wide and not too jagged. We'd lay out our clothes one by one—dungarees, shirt, underwear—soap them up, scrub them with the brush, turn them over and do the same thing.

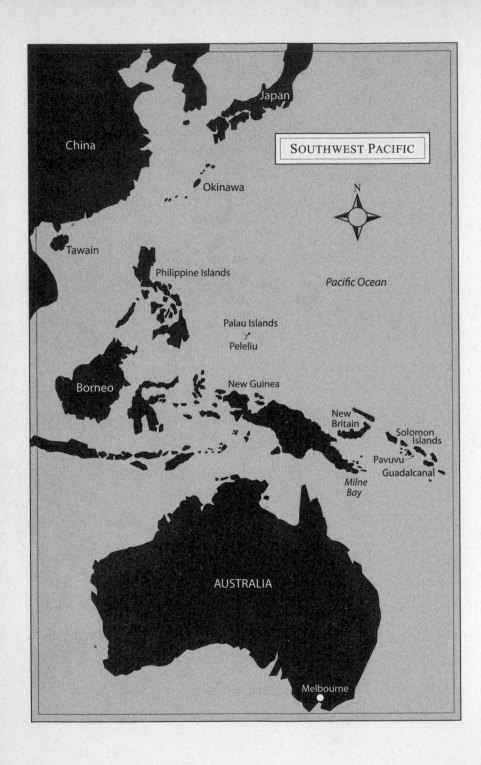

Then we'd rinse them in the running creek and lay them out to dry. If it was sunny, it didn't take too long. If it wasn't, we wore them wet.

We were never idle. We were learning the new art of jungle warfare, at it every day with mock combat or with marches, rifle range, pistol range.

In November, Third Battalion got a new commander, and we met him in a strange way. Lieutenant Colonel Austin Shofner had just come up from Australia, where he had been personally decorated by General Douglas MacArthur with the Distinguished Service Cross. In 1942 when he was a captain, Shofner was captured on Corregidor Island and survived the Bataan Death March. After almost a year in a prison camp, he and a dozen others—American Marines, soldiers, and sailors and Filipino soldiers—escaped into the jungle, where they joined local guerrillas to fight the Japs.

We were down in a creek bed shooting our .45s when someone came thrashing out of the underbrush and the vines. It was Colonel Shofner. He asked what we were doing, then told one of the guys, "Set me up a target."

We did so. He unholstered his .45 and shot one, two, three, four, five times, leaving a perfect V pattern over the bull's-eye. Then he stuck his pistol back into his holster and walked back into the jungle without a word. I think you could have taken a ruler and not a shot would have been out of line. I never will forget that.

We went on pulling maneuver after maneuver, but we hadn't prac-

ticed landings with the LSTs and LSMs—Landing Ships, Medium—
which for some reason were not yet available. Finally one afternoon
late in December we boarded DUKWs and started across the bay.

A DUKW—Ducks, we called them—is not much more than a low-
sided amphibious truck, about thirty feet long and a little over eight
feet wide. It could carry about twenty troops and was pretty smooth
and speedy on land but slow and rough-riding in the water. The only
time I ever got seasick was in a DUKW, and that day I was not the
only one.

Just as the mortar section was getting ready to board our DUKW
for an amphibious exercise, the wind and rain came up. That was nothing new to us. By the time we got out into the bay a gray curtain dropped
over us. We couldn't see thirty yards, much less the other DUKWs. Our
coxman lost his bearing, and then he lost his breakfast. I wasn't feeling
so good myself. A wave of seasickness swept over everybody. The diesel exhaust blowing in our faces only made it worse. Pretty soon we all
had our heads over the side. I think Jim Burke and P. A. Wilson were
the only men in that DUKW who didn't get sick.

In the middle of everything we got hung up on a reef. We sat in the
water going up and coming down, up and down, banging on that reef.
I thought, It's going to knock a hole in the bottom of this thing. We're
in trouble out here.

Fortunately DUKWs had a double hull. But for two hours we were
knocked around out in that bay. When we finally wallowed to shore,

some of the men were so sick they took them to the hospital on New Guinea.

On Christmas Eve we boarded the USS *Noel Palmer* and sailed a hundred miles or so up the coast to Oro Bay, the main supply base. The Seventh Marines had already been there and gone. Here we learned we were being held in reserve for the assault on Cape Gloucester, New Britain.

Four days later General William Rupertus, the commander in charge of the invasion, called for his reserves, and K Company, Third Battalion boarded LST 204. There were about 150 of us. None had set foot on an LST before—we hadn't trained on them. We walked up the ramp and they closed the big clamshell doors behind us, and off we sailed. I felt that we were like a boxer trained for his Friday night fight. We were ready. We had pulled enough maneuvers, done everything humanly possible to prepare every man for combat.

They'd started the invasion without us.

On the day after Christmas, while we were at Oro Bay, the Seventh Marines and the First and Second battalions of the Fifth Marines waded ashore on Cape Gloucester. Their objective was a Japanese airfield at the southwestern tip of New Britain. But instead of landing on the beach nearest the airfield, most of them had gone in several miles southeast, along the shores of Borgen Bay. This took the Japs by surprise, and our men landed without a shot being fired. But just beyond the narrow beach, where the invasion maps had indicated "damp flats," they ran into a wall of jungle and a swamp. The flats were damp, all right, up to the Marines' armpits.

Supplies from the LSTs piled up on the beaches as the Marines hacked and waded and swam through to solid land. Then they went on in driving rain to capture part of the airfield by December 30.

We landed the next morning, New Year's Day.

By then engineers had bulldozed a path across the swamp and laid down logs to make a corduroy road. Supplies were moving. We were scattered but we were able to get together pretty quickly, and next morning we started a sweep inland, moving south and west. The Seventh Marines were somewhere ahead of us and on our left. By late afternoon we had gone a few miles without encountering a single enemy. We stopped for the night and were just starting to dig in alongside a little creek when about fifteen Japs popped out of the jungle on the other side. They came splashing through the water and the high grass, bayonets raised over their heads and screaming *banzai!*

I had been carrying the mortar base plate and didn't have a rifle. I dropped the plate and pulled my .45 out quick—I don't even remember drawing it—and fired, catching one of them in the chest. He was about thirty-five or forty feet away from me, still running when he went down. Other Marines were firing right and left and more Japs were stumbling, going down. The rest turned back to the woods. I don't think more than one or two got away.

That was the first man I killed. I didn't feel anything but relief. He didn't get me. I got him.

After that episode, I always carried an M1 *and* my pistol. A pistol is fine if somebody's up close, but I didn't want anybody getting that close again. That attack broke me in right away.

We pulled off the creek and moved three hundred yards up a knoll and dug in again. It was a very nervous night. I couldn't see a thing. In the dark the land crabs came out and started rustling around in the leaves, and I was half convinced that the Japs were coming any minute. Everybody was a little trigger-happy anyway after the banzai charge. In the middle of the night one of the guys crawled out of his foxhole, probably to take a piss, and our sergeant, Johnny Marmet, shot him. He was wounded, not killed, but we had our first casualty.

At daybreak moisture was dripping off the leaves. Everything was soaked, and a kind of gray-blue haze hung in the air, a spooky mist that hid everything beyond the closest trees. It would be there almost every morning, especially after a rain. I never saw anything like it anywhere else and I never got used to it.

We started out again. We were picking our way south through thick jungle without finding any Japs when we came under fire on our left. It turned into a pretty good firefight until somebody up the line realized that we had run into the Seventh Marines, Third Battalion. Before we got it stopped, one of our men had been killed. It wasn't the only time we would encounter friendly fire, Marines shooting Marines. And when we did, it would again be from the Seventh Marines.

We had been advancing parallel to their Third Battalion when they had come up against a pocket of Japs that slowed them down. We went on without meeting any opposition and then began a swing back to the left. That's when we suddenly appeared on their right, and they opened fire.

We all finally caught up with a large body of Japs dug in along the far side of a stream we came to call Suicide Creek. They were screened behind brush, and every time we tried to wade across, they just cut us to pieces. We lost a lot of good men there.

Jim Burke and I were holed up some distance to the right of where the Seventh Marines were trying to cross. There was a small break in the trees, hardly big enough to call a clearing, and we'd set up a five-gallon water can with a canteen cup on top. I got thirsty and walked over to get a drink, all the time watching out for myself. After I put the cup back on top of the water can and ducked back, Jim went over for a drink. He was just reaching for that cup when there was a shot and the cup flew off into the brush. I felt something hit my sock just in front of my ankle. I looked down and there was a fragment of bullet stuck there, still hot.

Jim took three steps straight back and turned to me and grinned.

"I don't think I'm that thirsty," he said.

We knew whoever had fired at us was above our heads, somewhere in the trees, most likely tied in, as we'd learned from the Guadalcanal veterans. We crouched there for a while scanning the branches but all we could see was a green wall of foliage.

I went off to find K Company's .30-cal machine gunner.

"There's a Jap sniper up there somewhere, Norman," I told him. "He's well camouflaged, but we know he's there."

Norman set up his tripod and swiveled his gun upward and cut loose, raking the trees back and forth. Bits of leaf and falling branches showered down. There was a sudden crack and a body dropped out of the canopy and jerked to a stop about twenty feet above the ground. When we left he was swinging there upside down with his rifle dangling beneath him.

Farther down the line the Seventh Marines were still hung up at Suicide Creek. The Japs were invisible, dug in behind earth-and-log bunkers or behind the roots that fanned out like walls from the base of the tallest trees. Bazooka shells would bounce off the bunkers without detonating, and we couldn't use our mortars because of the forest canopy. The stream was about forty feet wide with steep banks. In the afternoon three Sherman tanks showed up, crashing through the underbrush, and stopped at the near edge of the stream. But the embankment was too steep, so a bulldozer was called forward to carve a ramp down to creek level. We heard later that a sniper shot the bulldozer driver out of his seat. Another Marine climbed up to take his place and he was shot, too. A third Marine ducked down behind the dozer and, somehow working the controls with a shovel and an ax handle, managed to finish the job. Next morning, January 4, the tanks churned across Suicide Creek and the Japs fell back and we all started moving forward again.

Those were the tactics the Japs would use over and over. They would set up and let us come to them. Then they'd retreat through the jungle and set up again farther on. We couldn't see them until we were right on top of them and they opened fire. Sometimes the undergrowth was so thick you couldn't see even three feet in front of you. You knew there was a Marine somewhere on your right and another on your left. But you couldn't see either one. That's a weird feeling when you're moving forward. I thought many times, Hell, I'm the only man out here. I'm fighting this war all by myself.

What the Guadalcanal veterans had said stuck in my mind. Watch your back. Watch your sides. Watch everywhere.

About this time we had our one and only problem on New Britain with Japanese aircraft. It was a small single-engine plane. We actually never saw him, but we heard him. We called him "Piss-call Charley" because he'd come over every night around one o'clock or two o'clock and drop a single bomb wherever he thought we were. It wasn't a very big bomb, about a hundred pounds. Just harassment, that's all. We could hear them firing at him over by the airfield with those twin 40s, but I don't think they ever hit him because the next night he was back again, right on schedule.

Then one night he came over and dropped his bomb and it went off real close, wounding several of our guys. One of them was in a foxhole with Jim Burke. Jim couldn't see in the darkness, but he knew the guy was badly wounded—he died later—and right away Burke yelled for a corpsman. Seconds later he yelled "Corpsman!" again. I could hear him every few seconds hollering for a corpsman, over and over.

It took a corpsman no more than a minute and a half to get to the foxhole. But afterward Jim said it felt like ten minutes. Combat would do that to you. Hours seemed to go by in minutes. Minutes would stretch out into hours.

―――――――

The farther we got from Suicide Creek, the stronger the resistance from the Japs. After we took a little knob called Hill 150, they wounded our battalion commander, Lieutenant Colonel David McDougal. Then they got McDougal's executive officer, Major Joseph Skoczylas. So on January 8 we had a new battalion commander, Lieutenant Colonel Lewis Walt.

We were fighting uphill now, advancing in a wide arc through the jungle. It was raining, always raining. Every stream was swollen and the ground was gumbo. Moving forward was like trying to walk through oatmeal. I was still carrying around that mortar base plate, but we couldn't use it much because of the trees, so 90 percent of the time I took my place up front with the riflemen.

Colonel Walt was looking for a location identified on a document they'd taken from a dead Jap. It was called Aogiri Ridge, and it was apparently very important to the Japs, because the document warned that the ridge must be held at any cost. All evening we slogged on, dragging a .37 artillery piece that was our only heavy weapon. We'd load it with grapeshot or armor-piercing shells, depending on what we were faced with. From time to time we'd stop and fire it to clear out a machine-gun nest or a bunker. As we set up they'd fire at us and the bullets would sing off the quarter-inch steel shield on the front of the gun. We took turns, five or six of us at a time, wrestling that rascal up the hill in the mud. I pushed part of the way, slipping and sliding, vines snatching at my boots. As a reward they let me fire it. By dark we were sitting along the crest of a ridge, exhausted and facing a line of Jap bunkers. As we were digging in we could hear them in front of us, a dozen or so yards away.

After dark they started yelling at us. About ten thirty, one of them got out in front calling, "Raider! Raider! Why you no fire? Why you no fire?"

Raider was our machine-gun sergeant.

In a calm, quiet voice, Raider told his gunner, "Give him a short burst, about two hundred rounds." And he did. That Jap was very quiet after that.

About an hour and a half past midnight, they came screaming at us through the rain, hollering "Marine, you die!" I was in a foxhole with Jim Burke. I'd had bayonet drill in boot camp along with everyone else, but I'd made up my mind that as long as I had ammunition I wasn't going to let anyone get close enough to use my bayonet. But I saw a Jap silhouetted at the edge of the foxhole. I was on my knees with my rifle pointed at him and I shoved my bayonet into his chest as hard and deep as I could, right beneath the breastbone. In one motion I leveraged him off the ground and swung him over my shoulder, pulling the trigger all the way. I don't know how many shots I put into him—four or five anyway.

He was dead when he landed.

We fought off the charge, and then there was silence, except for the *pit-pat* of the rain. Then they charged again. And again. We were running low on ammo and we were holding our fire until they were almost on top of us. All the time Colonel Walt in the command post about fifty yards back was calling in long-range artillery, which was crashing almost in our faces.

It was one of those shells that got Lonnie Howard—the guy I mentioned earlier who had a premonition and asked me to keep his wristwatch.

That night we took five banzai charges. In the half-light of morning we could see Japs sprawled everywhere. In some places you could have stepped from body to body without touching the ground. Bleary-eyed and weary, we wandered out and counted more than two hundred. The rest had slipped away in the darkness. After a nerve-wracking fight, we had Aogiri Ridge to ourselves.

Now I was glad that I was carrying an M1. Most mortarmen carried the lighter carbines, but a carbine couldn't stop a charging Jap.

After that night of banzai attacks, Jim and I were moved down to the extreme right end of the line. There wasn't anybody beyond us. It's a funny feeling when you know you don't have any support on your flank. If you ever needed a guy who was calm and knew what the hell he was doing in a situation like that, it was Jim Burke. Whether you were with Jim in a foxhole or out in the open you knew he had your back covered.

The next night I spotted a Jap a few yards off trying to sneak around behind us. All I could see was a dark shape moving through the trees. I grabbed my M1 and shot him. He must have been a scout because he was alone.

I also almost shot a Marine.

We were digging a foxhole. I was standing guard and Jim was digging—one man always stands guard while the other digs. You always throw the dirt out in front of you to build up a little rampart. I could see somebody crawling toward us through the underbrush. I reached over and pushed Jim's helmet down and laid my .45 up on top of that mound of fresh dirt. I didn't know if it was a Jap or a Marine coming, but I knew I had him either way. When he got about two feet from me, I could see the silhouette of a Marine helmet.

"Pssst, Burgin," he said. "You got any water?"

I recognized the voice.

"Yeah, Oswalt. I've got some water."

I handed him the canteen and he took a long drink.

I waited until he was finished.

"Oswalt," I said, "what the hell are you doing out of that foxhole? Do you know I almost shot you right between the eyes?"

He stared at me.

"Let me tell you something," I said. "You get out of that damn foxhole again tonight, I *will* shoot you just on general principles."

Later they renamed the ridge we were on Walt's Ridge. And we found out why it was so important to the Japs. Their main supply trail up from Borgen Bay lay just beyond, and that trail led straight west through the jungle to their main headquarters. It was the key to their whole operation.

We were left to mop up the ridge and the Seventh Marines' Third Battalion fought its way up another high point, Hill 660. After that they gave us all a rest. We'd been at it for two weeks.

From that point on the Japs were finished on New Britain. There was no place for them to go except east through the jungle, back to their big naval base at Rabaul—and our planes had bombed that into uselessness.

We had plenty of fighting ahead of us. But for now, we came out of the jungle down to the edge of the airfield, which was in our hands, and went into reserve. It scarcely seemed possible, but the rains started

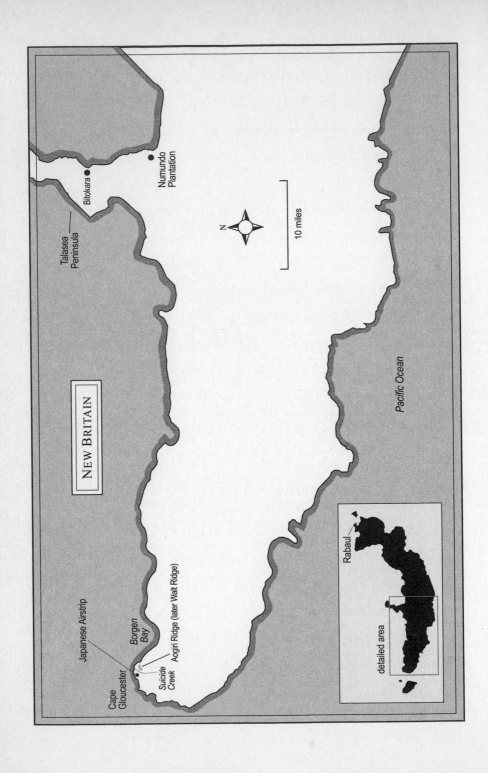

NEW BRITAIN

Talasea
Peninsula

Bitokara

Numundo
Plantation

N

10 miles

Japanese Airstrip

Cape
Gloucester

Borgen
Bay

Suicide
Creek

Aogiri Ridge (later Walt Ridge)

Pacific Ocean

Rabaul

detailed area

coming harder, thirty-six inches in one twenty-four-hour period. I'd never seen so much rain. We stayed wet so long my little toenails rotted off. Our clothes mildewed and stank. *We* stank. The only time we could bathe or wash our clothes was if we crossed a stream or found ourselves near the ocean.

The Marine Corps had discovered the convenience of hammocks. You'd tie them between two trees and they'd keep you out of the mud—if the rain hadn't rotted the strings. Sometimes at night you'd hear a *rip* and a *splat* and a lot of cussing. If it was raining you could drape a rubber tarp over you to keep dry, and you'd have a net to keep off the mosquitoes. You had to zip it open to get in and out.

Sometimes the zipper didn't work fast enough.

New Britain was crawling with land crabs. After the first few weeks we had a new man join us on the island, George Sarrett. George was from Dennison, Texas, and I don't believe George was afraid of anybody or anything. Not the Japs, not the Devil himself. But a land crab could run him off the face of the earth. George was sound asleep in his hammock one day. The land crabs were scrabbling around and I picked one up and slipped it into George's hammock. He had his trousers on but no shirt. It wasn't long before that land crab had skittered up his trousers and out across his chest.

Sarrett came out of there with his KA-BAR knife, slashing that mosquito net from one end to the other. Just—*whoosh*—and he was out of that hammock. Didn't make a sound.

I never did tell him who put that land crab in his hammock.

I thought the mosquitoes were worse than the land crabs. We joked that the big ones would hold you down while the little ones sucked you dry. We had a mosquito repellant but it was absolutely pungent. You'd pour a little bit out of a bottle into the palm of your hands and spread it around. It would keep the mosquitoes off, but you could hardly live with yourself. It was hard to tell what was worse, the mosquitoes or the smell.

We were also fighting a more serious problem. We called it "jungle rot." It was a fungus that would invade your armpits, ankles and crotch, and spread beneath your belt. Damp underwear seemed to promote the fungus, so some stopped wearing underpants—those whose underpants hadn't already rotted off. The only thing that would relieve the itch was gentian violet, an antifungal medication. The corpsmen would paint all the places you'd scratched raw and the festering rash of pimples under your arms. Everybody had that purple stuff on them. We were a colorful mess.

But at least we were out of combat. We cooked pancakes over an open fire, and I was able to go swimming in the ocean a couple times. It got deep pretty fast twenty-five or thirty yards out. I dove to the bottom and looked around. There were a lot of shells and starfish scattered on the ocean floor, things that seemed strange and wonderful to a boy from an east Texas farm.

One day we were washing our clothes in the ocean and I waded out to where it was waist deep. I looked up and here came two Jap bodies floating along. I guess they'd been killed on airplanes or ships. We got out of the water pretty fast then.

———————

The Japs had pretty much melted into the jungle. In February we climbed into LCMs and made a series of landings eastward along the coast from Borgen Bay. We hoped to catch up with the Japs and cut off their retreat to Rabaul. We'd land and conduct a patrol for a day or two, searching jungle trails for signs of the enemy. Then we'd move on, leap-frogging another unit that had landed farther up the coast.

We found a few stragglers. They'd leave two or three behind with knee mortars and a machine gun. We called them knee mortars because they had a folding arch that looked like it could fit over your knee. They wouldn't use it that way, of course, because there was too much kick—it would break a man's leg—but we called it that anyway.

When we'd come up on the Japs they'd open fire. If we didn't get them, they'd move farther up the trail and set up again. By late in the month we'd captured a major enemy supply dump, meeting only occasional resistance.

When we went on patrol we'd take along war dogs that could sniff out Japs. After a while I realized that I could smell the Japs, too, if they were in the area and the wind was right. It was just like hunting in the woods back home, when I could smell a squirrel or a deer. But the smell of Japs was completely different from anything I'd ever smelled. They told us they could smell us, too. They said we smelled like goats.

We'd have a dog with us, and the Japs would be sleeping in these A-frame lean-tos they made of palm leaves. And the dog would get you in real close, like a bird dog. Japs would be inside, napping or just lying around.

We'd go in both ends at once and bayonet them or slit their throats. We didn't want to shoot them and let anybody else in the vicinity know we were around.

The first time we went out on patrol we captured three and took them all the way back to battalion headquarters. By then the rain had rotted out our shoes and our clothes were just about falling off our backs.

At the battalion they gave our prisoners fresh underwear and socks, new shoes, new caps, new dungarees, the works. Here we were, wearing the same underwear and socks and shoes for thirty or forty days. We thought, To hell with this. They're giving the Japs all that, but they won't give us anything. So we fixed it. We didn't bring in any more prisoners.

In early March, hoping to cut off the Japs once and for all, the Fifth Marines made a major landing on the west side of the Talasea Peninsula, a long finger of land sticking out about 120 miles into the Bismarck Sea east of Borgen Bay. The Third Battalion was in reserve again. We missed the main landing but sailed around the northern tip of the peninsula, and the next afternoon came ashore on the eastern side, where we relieved the First Battalion.

From what I could see, Talasea was a couple volcanic peaks overlooking abandoned coconut plantations. The Japs had built a small airstrip near the shore, and there was a Jap fighter plane on its back in the middle of the runway. Farther inland at a place called Bitokara there was a German Lutheran mission, also abandoned. The Fifth Regiment had set up headquarters there after driving off the Japs, and we were assigned to guard the headquarters. The defenders had put up a brief fight, killing eight Marines and losing 150 of their own. Then they had moved out.

On March 12, we raised the flag over the mission, the same flag raised in January over the air base at Cape Gloucester. In the three battles I fought during the war, that was the only flag I ever saw raised in victory. When that flag went up I thought, God, I'm glad I'm an American. I had participated in raising the flag in high school a few times. I always felt honored to do that. But seeing that flag go up at Talasea was a different feeling altogether. It was like the feeling you get whenever they play "Taps." You know—Old Glory.

For the next month and a half the three battalions of the Fifth Marines would scour Talasea Peninsula and beyond, looking for the Japs. K Company was sent south from the mission at Bitokara toward a place on the map called Numundo Plantation, at the base of the peninsula. It was supposed to be a three-day patrol.

We had those little spotter planes—we called them grasshoppers—to help us off and on. One afternoon I saw a Japanese Zero get after one of those planes. The grasshopper was flying along the edge of the ocean, about fifty miles an hour or so. When the Zero showed up, the spotter plane dipped down to tree level and started weaving back and forth. The Zero must have been going more than a hundred, and he couldn't adjust. He made a pass at that little plane moving in slow motion and overshot his target and went flying by. Then he came around and made another pass—he missed again. As we watched he made pass after pass firing at the grasshopper, which kept zigzagging frantically. Finally I guess the Zero ran out of ammunition and flew off. Never did hit him. We were cheering for that little plane until he flew out of sight.

We were out more than ten days. And every day, it seemed, we would run into an ambush. As usual they'd leave a few guys behind with knee mortars and a machine gun. Before we could flank them they'd disappear. It was just aggravating. The few we came upon were in about as bad a shape as we were in, and they'd been there a lot longer. They were sick with malaria and were starving. Their wounds weren't healing. We tried to take them with us, but sometimes we had to leave them behind.

Along the way we ran into groups of dark-skinned natives who had come down out of the mountains, where they'd been hiding out with their wives and children after the Japs had started raiding their villages and plundering their gardens. Whenever we needed working parties they were there, about fifteen or twenty of them ready to carry ammunition and supplies.

Every so often we came upon a deserted village or coconut plantation. At one of them I saw this kid who looked like he could have been twelve to fifteen years old, maybe sixteen. It was hard to tell. He put his hands and feet on a coconut tree, with a machete tied around his waist, and he just walked up that thing. Climbed all the way to the top with his hands and feet. When he got to the top he took his machete and lopped the coconuts off. Then he came down the same way he went up.

We didn't eat a lot of coconuts, but we'd slash the ends of them off and drink the milk and throw the rest away.

One afternoon we stopped in a clearing around an abandoned hut. Some of our guys went to fill their canteens down by a creek, where the Japs opened up with machine guns. Everybody got the hell out of there, but they may have hit a couple of natives.

Later in the evening we were digging foxholes and the Japs started shelling us with knee mortars. We started digging faster. The natives grabbed sticks, tin can lids, or chunks of metal, or used just their hands, and started digging a long trench about a foot to eighteen inches deep. They were digging faster than we were with our entrenching tools. When they finished they just lay down in that thing, head to foot, head to foot.

We moved on, continuing to encounter rain-swollen streams. The wider ones we would follow down to the beach, where the flood had pushed up an apron of sand, and we'd wade across in the shallow water. A tree had fallen across one stream and we could hang on to the branches to cross over. Most of us had made it to the other side when the man in front of me, Andrew Geglein, slipped and went down on the upstream side. He disappeared into the chocolate-colored water with his rifle and all of his gear, just vanished. We thought he'd be washed underneath the fallen tree, and one of the guys got in on that side and searched along the log, and then farther downstream. Time was of the essence. Then another guy jumped in on the upstream side and groped along until he found Andrew hung up on the branches underneath. We hauled him up out of the water, but he was already gone.

I thought, That's a terrible way to lose your life when you're fighting a war.

After ten days out on patrol we got word to return to Bitokara. I don't know why, and I don't know what happened, but we were glad to get out. We just hauled ass. By then we had a lot of men wounded and a lot of men killed. I figure we were down to about three-quarters of a company. Around 235 men went in and about 175 or 180 came out.

It was the last combat we were to see on New Britain.

I had a souvenir to take with me. I had found a fine hara-kiri knife, a beautiful thing with an ivory handle and sheath.

Hara-kiri—they would do that. About thirty yards beyond one of the creeks we'd crossed, we came upon a Jap officer lying on his back with his knees up. I don't know whether he had been standing or kneeling when he had stabbed himself, but he had a bayonet stuck in his belly, and his hands were still curled around the grip. We didn't know how long he had been there. His face and body were black and bloated. I didn't take that bayonet.

Somebody else beat me to it.

———————

After we came off the Numundo patrol we hung around Bitokara for a month. The mission was on a hill overlooking a small harbor, where we swam and fished. There were broad lawns and flowers and fruit trees, including a pepper tree. I'd never seen one before. It was about eight or ten feet high and absolutely loaded with those little tabasco peppers. We also saw banana trees, though no bananas. Nearby there was a native village. The place must have been a tropical paradise before the war.

We swam in the local hot springs, in water as clear and soothing as in a bathtub. For most of us it was the first hot bath we'd had since Melbourne.

But the food situation didn't improve that much. There was never enough of it. About a month or so after we'd landed they brought out hot field-cooked meals to the front lines. There was a little piece of ham about three inches wide and a quarter inch thick, some potatoes, some cabbage. And a big navel orange. I looked at my mess tin and thought, What the hell? Do they think they're feeding a canary?

And do you know? I couldn't eat all of it. My stomach had shrunk so much, I could not clean my plate. I saved the orange for later on but I never did eat it. I went into New Britain weighing 180 pounds. I came out weighing 140.

We'd go in for lunch and they'd serve soup so thin you could read a newspaper through it. At night we'd designate one man to go down to the chow dump, where they stockpiled all the food, and he'd bring something back to the battalion, a gallon can of peaches or fruit cocktail or something like that. Everybody got their canteens out to have some, including our lieutenant. I'll call him "Legs," because he was a tall, gawky guy.

I guess we weren't the only ones raiding the chow dump, because headquarters finally came out with an order that anyone caught stealing food would be court-martialed.

When that order came down, Legs called us together and chewed our butts. He got real indignant about the whole thing. "*You* guys are going to have to stop stealing that food! They're going to court-martial *your* ass!" A real big shot.

He had eaten as much of that fruit as anyone else. I thought, What kind of officer is this? So afterward I said to the guys, "Don't pay any attention. Let's go ahead and take the food, but make damn sure we don't get caught. Whenever it comes into camp, we just won't let him know it's here and he won't get any more."

And we did, and he didn't.

It was not the last time I was to get crossways with Lieutenant Legs.

In our last days on New Britain, the Navy established a PT base on Talasea to keep after Jap barge traffic along the coast. I loved those PT boats, and I wasn't alone. We'd all go down and visit with the crews and swap lies, always trying to outdo one another. They'd invite us on board and we'd sit at the turrets and fire the guns. Get a feel for what it was like to be on one of those things. One of our guys, Fred Miller, went out on patrol with them one day, and when he got back, our captain gave him hell.

He said, "Miller, if you're going to get your ass killed, I'd prefer you do it fighting with the Marines."

Near the end of April LCMs carried the First and Third battalions back down the coast to Borgen Bay. Ten days later, about the first of May, they started shipping units out on LSTs. On May 4, the Third Battalion mustered down at the beach and, after waiting around for an hour or so as usual, dragged ourselves aboard the USS *Elmore*, an attack transport.

We must have been the very last Marines to leave New Britain.

The division had been battered pretty badly. We'd lost 1,347 men. Those of us who were left had oozing red rashes from jungle rot, or dysentery—"the shits"—or malaria.

We'd all heard we were headed back to Melbourne, and I prayed I would soon see Florence again.

We were in for an unpleasant surprise.

CHAPTER 4

First Battle of Pavuvu

So we were at sea again. The scuttlebutt was already circulating a day or two out when the USS *Elmore*'s loudspeaker squawked to life and confirmed the bad news. We weren't going back to Australia. We would disembark at a place we'd never heard of—Pavuvu, in the Russell Islands.

Before long we'd all wish we'd never heard of Pavuvu and would never hear of it again.

The story was that some Army officers had picked out the island from the air. Never set a foot on it. They were flying around in a little spotter plane and they looked down and saw the neat rows of palm trees. And somebody said, "Yup, this'll do." Just decided then and there that Pavuvu was where we'd be going for rehab and retraining.

Later we found out that we couldn't blame it on the Army. One of our own had chosen Pavuvu—Major General Roy S. Geiger, commander of the Third Amphibious Corps. Guadalcanal was just sixty miles east. But Geiger didn't want us there after what had happened to the Third Marine Division: after Bougainville they'd been sent to Guadalcanal for R & R, and the island command had run the men absolutely ragged on work parties. They were too worn out to fight.

So Pavuvu was it for us.

At first it didn't look so bad. We pulled in late on May 7, 1944, and anchored in Macquitti Bay. From the deck of the *Elmore* we could see palm trees, a lagoon and sandy beaches. We didn't get to disembark until the next morning, in the kind of rain we thought we'd left behind on New Britain. That's when we got a close look at our new home.

The Navy's construction battalions, the Seabees, had been there, but they hadn't done much. There was one pier and a muddy road gouged through the palms. The flat part of the island, about six hundred acres, was covered by layers of rotten coconuts, and beneath that was mud. The place had been a plantation until the war started, when the people who owned and worked it took off. Ever since, those coconuts had been falling off the trees and rotting on the ground. Every now and then you'd hear one hit with a *thwack!* You learned to give the trees a wide berth. The smell was overwhelming. It was years before I could eat coconut again in any form.

Since the Seabees hadn't finished the job, the first arrivals had to build the camp. They found the tents and cots piled on the beach, most of them soaked through by the rains. The ones on the bottom of the piles were moldy. Some of the cots would come apart in your hands. The bivouac areas were ankle-deep in slop. The new guys stood in the rain, patching the holes in the tents, trying to get a footing, trying to find a dry place to pound in the tent stakes, only to see them float away. There were no wooden platforms—there were never any platforms beneath our tents, from start to finish—and when you'd lie down on the cots they'd sink into the mud like they had on New Britain. Some of the men decided to hell with it and strung hammocks between palm trees.

By the time we got there things had improved a little. The six-man pyramid tents were up, but they were full of holes. There was still plenty of mud and rotting coconuts around and there wasn't any electricity anywhere on the island, so we had no lights. Marines can improvise under any circumstances. We rounded up tin cans and bottles, filled them with sand, poured in gasoline, inserted a piece of rope and rigged up lamps. They started fires here and there, but at least we had enough light to read or write letters, which was all there was to do for a time.

Worse than the rotting coconuts, the rain, and the mud were the rats and the land crabs. They had pretty much taken over the place.

You'd see and hear the rats mostly at night, skittering across the tents or sliding down the tent ropes. They lived in the tops of the palm trees, where it was almost impossible to get at them.

We'd encountered land crabs before, but here they were absolutely everywhere. They were about the size of a fist, and their black and blue color reminded me of a bruise. I'd get up in the morning and they'd be down in my boots. I'd shake them and two or three would fall out and go scuttling sideways across the floor of the tent. They'd get into our clothes, they'd get into our bedclothes. Some of the guys got so aggravated that one Sunday morning they went on a land crab roundup, gathering them by the hundreds and dumping them in the street, where they poured gasoline over them and set them on fire. The stink from the burning crabs made us forget the rotting coconuts for a while.

During the days, work details went out to scoop up the layers of coconuts and truck them to a swamp. After we came off New Britain we had added one gun to the mortars and I was made corporal, so I was exempt. But I sent out my share of those work details. Everyone would come back stinking of sour coconut milk. There was no running water on the island, and you'd see somebody standing out in the daily downpour with a bar of good Marine soap and a brush, hoping to scrub off the smell before the rain stopped. The rain always started at the same time. You could set your watch by it. But it stopped without a warning, like somebody turned off a big faucet in the sky. Even after such a "shower," the stink of coconuts never seemed to go away.

When we weren't moving coconuts, we had parties hauling crushed coral to pave the roads and lanes between the tents, trying to keep on top of the mud. We'd also fill our helmets with crushed coral and carry it in a bucket brigade to make a dry floor under our cots. If you could find a couple scraps of wood you were a rich man. You could put up a dry platform where you could stow your clothes and shoes and letters from home. I salvaged a board or two and propped up Florence's photo. Guys were always showing off their girlfriends' pictures, but I wanted to keep Florence to myself.

A week or so after I arrived at Pavuvu, my mail caught up to me. My sister Ila sent me a package of homemade strawberry jam and some cookies. They were all broken up in transit, but even the crumbs tasted good. Best of all, I got a bundle of letters from my precious Florence. I sat down and read them right away. I was also writing her whenever I had the time to spare. It cost seventy cents to send an airmail letter to Australia. Surface mail was free. Even though I was making only sixty-four dollars a month, I sent them by air as often as I could.

Florence wrote that she was still working at the biscuit factory in Melbourne, putting in long hours. Her little brother—the one Jim Burke and I had carried piggyback on the Melbourne train platform—had chicken pox, but he was getting better. She told me she loved me and was waiting for my return.

I missed her terribly. Memories of the things we'd talked about and done together in Melbourne kept coming back. Our walks through the park full of flowers, buying fresh fruit from the little stand at Young & Jackson, just sitting on a bench in the sun. At night, lying in the tent, I'd think of the kisses we'd stolen. Or the times she teased me. Or my twenty-first birthday, when I drank a little too much and we sat in the dark movie theater and she cradled my spinning head in her arms and kept kissing me. Now my heart ached for her, and I wondered if I'd been wrong, if we should have got married when we had the chance, before I shipped out.

They cleared out some palm trees and hung up a sheet and started showing movies two or three nights a week. We sat on coconut logs, which cut into your backside after an hour or two. But those movies helped take our minds off things. We shouted advice to actors who seemed especially dumb around women—"Kiss her, you idiot!"—and whenever a pretty starlet appeared we'd yell and whistle at the projectionist to back up the film and show the scene again.

We no longer had to eat out in the rain or in our tents. They had battalion galleys up and working and screened against mosquitoes, which were everywhere. We were supposed to be taking the little yellow Atabrine pills to prevent malaria, but not everybody was going along with it. They tasted bitter, they turned your skin yellow, and there was a rumor going around that they'd make you sterile. In the mornings when we lined up in front of the tents for roll call, a corpsman would walk down the line. We'd be ordered to open our mouths—wide—and he'd toss that pill in as far back as he could get it. We got our Atabrine whether we wanted it or not.

We still had no fresh meat, no fresh eggs, no fresh anything. Every now and then a ship pulled in from Banika, the supply island between Pavuvu and Guadalcanal. But we had no refrigeration and couldn't keep anything perishable very long in the heat and humidity. The cooks managed to bake bread, but by the time it got to us the weevils had moved in. I guess they added some protein to our diet. Mostly we lived on heated C rations, which provided three daily meals in one carton. There was always Spam or some kind of potted meat-and-vegetable stew. These were greasy when warm and congealed when cold. There was always a can of crackers and a little cup of cheese you could spread. There were powdered eggs and powdered potatoes, and a powder that made up into a urine-colored lemonade we called "battery acid." You could drink it, or you could use it to scrub down the deck.

But little by little we all started to put on weight.

A few weeks after we settled in, a transport arrived with the Forty-sixth Replacement Battalion, fresh men from the States. Many of the old Guadalcanal veterans turned in their gear and lined up to go home. They'd earned it. The First Division band assembled down at the dock and played them off with "California Here I Come," ending, as always, with the "Marines' Hymn." There wasn't a dry eye in the place.

Among the replacements who marched ashore was a young private first class, Gene Sledge. He was assigned to my mortar platoon. We'd soon be calling him "Sledgehammer." Sledge was a little older than the other recruits. I learned later he had a couple years of college behind him, but to me he was just another kid, wet behind the ears. Those of us who had been on New Britain were a sorry-looking bunch, yellow from the Atabrine tablets, skin like leather—they didn't call us Leathernecks for nothing. We were still skin and bones compared to the guys from stateside. I think our appearance shocked our replacements, and maybe gave them a little taste of what they'd look like, too, after combat.

Right away we sent the newcomers out on work details, hauling coconuts and coral. The first week or two you'd hear them bellyache about this and that. The food or the land crabs or the rotting coconuts and mud. I didn't have much sympathy. I had just come off of four months of battle, where I was sleeping in foxholes when it would be raining and I'd wake up the next morning with water up to my chin. They'd been sleeping on momma's white sheets in Marine Corps barracks. Now they thought they'd fallen into the hellhole of creation, and I guess from their point of view they had. That's certainly what Sledge felt years later when he wrote about the experience in *With the Old Breed*, one of the great combat books of the war.

Overseas Marines and stateside Marines are two different breeds almost. We were a lot more relaxed as far as discipline. We didn't go in for much of that parade stuff like they did back in the States. But we did calisthenics, and some mornings after roll call we'd fall out and run three miles before breakfast. We had a large field where we played baseball and volleyball. We went to the rifle range.

One thing I want to clear up.

You read in books about suicides on Pavuvu. Someone would get a Dear John letter, and there'd be a shot some night and later everyone would learn he'd put a rifle in his mouth and pulled the trigger.

I think that's a crock. I was in the Marine Corps, in the First Marine Division, from 1943 until 1945 and I know of only one suicide in that span. There were always rumors, especially on Pavuvu. For a while somebody was supposedly going around and knifing people at night. Just creep into your tent and slit your throat and vanish. That rumor got thick and heavy.

The funny thing was, it never happened *here*. It always happened somewhere else. There was no evidence that this was happening anywhere. But the rumors got pretty strong, and spread and grew from there. And to tell the truth, we all got a little edgy.

There was a guy named Al Flame. About the time the rumors of the knifings were going around, he was visiting somebody else's tent in the next company over—Marines were always socializing from tent to tent at night. One evening, instead of going around the end of the tent rows and bypassing K Company, he decided to cut through. We'd heard all the stories. It was pitch dark when I spotted someone moving among the tents. I pulled my .45 and stuck it in his face and challenged him.

"You take another step and I'll blow your head off."

"Burgin," he said. "This is me! Al Flame, dammit!"

I just said okay. Al went on about his business and I went on about mine. But it shows our frame of mind.

We called it "Going Asiatic." Going crazy.

Sergeant Elmo Haney was the most Asiatic Marine I knew. He had been in the Corps since World War I and he'd seen it all. He was a platoon sergeant assigned to K Company, but he didn't have a job—a platoon sergeant without a platoon. Sergeant Haney had gone Asiatic. He would do something wrong, what he imagined was some infraction, and he'd assign himself Extra Police Duty. He'd put on a full combat pack and march down the street muttering to himself, and at the end of the street he'd put himself through a full bayonet drill, all by himself.

You'd see him in the shower scrubbing all over his body with that Marine brush, even his testicles. And I mean those bristles were *tough*.

We'd heard they had stationed him back home once, and he had gone AWOL. He'd gone down to the docks and caught a freighter to the Pacific and worked his way back to K Company.

After Peleliu he went home for good. I heard he told someone, "This is a young man's war."

―――――――

About this time I started having trouble with our platoon leader again, the officer we called Lieutenant Legs. The truth is, a lot of us had been having trouble with Lieutenant Legs since the canned peaches incident on New Britain.

As usual, Legs was making up the rules as he went along. We'd made a practice beach landing and gone in. He told us where to set up the mortars, and we did. Pretty soon a battalion commander came along.

"Who the hell set these up?" he barked at Legs. "Why did you set them up *there*?" Just chewed up his butt.

After he was gone, Legs started chewing me out. "What the hell were you thinking, setting up that way?" he yelled. "They're supposed to be over there!"

He was getting worse. He'd tell us to do something and then he'd chew our ass for doing what he said. It was demoralizing. Our platoon sergeant, Johnny Marmet, knew something was wrong. Finally he called the mortar section together.

"All right, there's something going on around here and I want to know what the hell it is."

He went down the line, asking each man if he had a gripe. "Whatever the hell is on your mind, I want to hear it."

Some didn't have a problem with Legs. But some of us definitely did. I was the last one. Marmet dismissed everybody else. I was sitting there, and he said, "Burgin, what is it? What's going on in this outfit?"

"John, Legs has been riding us for the stuff he's been doing ever since New Britain," I said. "He's passing down the blame to me and everybody else for his own damn mistakes. I'm going to tell you something, John. You get that son of a bitch off of my ass or *I'm* going to get him off. And if I get him off, both of us are going to be sorry."

Marmet just said, "I'll take care of it."

And he did, I guess. Because after that Lieutenant Legs didn't give me any more problems for a long time.

A sergeant could do that—you'd better believe it. The first sergeant, gunny sergeant, he pretty well runs the company. Whatever he said went.

He'd just say, "Lieutenant, I need to have a word with you." A wise lieutenant would listen. Because if he didn't the sergeant would go to the captain and say, "Hey, we have a problem with Lieutenant So-and-So. This is what he's doing, and it's not right. And he's not listening to me."

Before long it would be fixed. The word of a sergeant carried a lot of weight. Yes, it did.

I had no trouble with other officers. Sledge, in his book *With the Old Breed*, was too hard on officers, in my opinion. But even Sledge liked Hillbilly Jones. We *all* liked Hillbilly.

First Lieutenant Edward A. Jones had been with us on New Britain, and he would be with us on Peleliu, for a time. He was the most—I don't know what the word is—*disciplinary* officer I was ever around. He wasn't a horse's patoot. He didn't make up his own rules. He went by the book. His mind-set was, You're a Marine, and you're going to act like a Marine whether you're in the States or out here in combat. That's the way it's going to be.

Whenever we'd fall in for morning roll call, standing in ranks, he'd be out in front and he'd inspect the rifles. He'd spent five years as a seagoing Marine, so he was sharp. I mean he would pull that rifle—*snap!*—and twirl it—*snap!*—and it would come back to you—*snap!* He had it all. When you fell in, your collar was buttoned, your cuffs were buttoned. You stood erect. You didn't slouch. You stood like a *Marine.* From reveille to recall in the afternoon he was as GI as they ever came, I'll guarantee you.

But after recall turned us loose at four o'clock, Hillbilly was a different human being. He'd wander down to our tents carrying the guitar he always had with him and sit around and we'd sing and shoot the bull all night. Coming over from New Britain, we'd gather around Hillbilly on the deck of the *Elmore* singing one song after another. "Waltzing Matilda" was popular, from our stay in Melbourne. We sang "Danny Boy," and "She's Nobody's Darling But Mine." My own favorite was "San Antonio Rose."

For some reason I always thought Hillbilly was from West Virginia, because he knew every country and western song. The fact of it is, he was from Red Lion, Pennsylvania, right on the Maryland border. Hillbilly was the leader of K Company's machine-gun platoon, and the kind of officer you always wanted to have somewhere near you in a battle. He was soft-spoken, always calm and reassuring. Nothing rattled him.

When everybody else was sweating and filthy, Hillbilly always looked fresh scrubbed. None of us knew how he did it.

They were working us harder now. More marches, more drills, more inspections. We all knew they were getting us ready for something, toughening us up. In July signs appeared in the galleys: KILL JAPS! KILL JAPS! We'd heard Colonel Lewis "Chesty" Puller posted them. He'd lost a brother in the fighting on Guam.

We were pulling more maneuvers. Just at the squad level first, then working up to platoons, and finally companies. You couldn't maneuver with anything larger than a company on Pavuvu. The island was only ten miles long and six miles wide. There was a low hill in the center, covered with jungle. That didn't leave much wiggle room for fifteen thousand Marines and their weapons to pull maneuvers at the same time. One unit would be doing close-order drill and another would come along and march right through it, neither paying any attention to the other. The weapons ranges were in constant use, always some unit waiting to get on. If they ever lined all of us up to hike, we were sure the front of the column would come right up to the back of the column. We'd be like a snake chasing its tail.

After breakfast most mornings the mortar section would go out for a training exercise. We wanted to teach the new guys just as the Guadalcanal veterans had taught us. We showed them what to do and what not to do in combat, we told them what to look for, all the Jap tricks. We'd work on how and where to set up the guns. We'd have them humping ammunition. Of course they'd been through it all before at boot camp. They knew the routine. But we'd practice it, carry it out and practice it again.

I don't know who in the Marines dreams up all that stuff in your training. Like jerking you out of your sleep and doing a forced run or a forced march. But they do a very good job of it. I don't think I can stress it too much: They don't only train you physically. They train you mentally. They know if they can make you upset about something, if they can aggravate you, they're getting you in the right frame of mind for combat. They throw something unexpected into the agenda, so that when you get on the battlefield you're already mad. You're ready to get out of all that you've been going through, all that BS you've been doing. You're ready to kill someone.

Some thought it was all BS, the whole four months we spent on that island. I wasn't on the same page with a lot of guys who downgrade Pavuvu. When you look back on it, the Marines knew what they were doing. We were glad when it was over, even though we knew we were facing death where we were going. In a way, anything would have been better than Pavuvu.

———————

Around July 4 a few of us caught a break.

Captain Andrew Allison Haldane—we called him "Ack-Ack" on account of his initials—called nine or ten of us in. He had a special assignment for us. Besides myself, there was Hillbilly Jones, John Teskevich, Jim Day, George Sarrett, Paul R. Yarborough, P. A. Wilson and a few others.

Captain Haldane had been K/3/5's commander the night we fought off five banzai charges on New Britain. They'd awarded him the Silver Star for that. He was as well liked as any officer I knew. I never heard him raise his voice at any man. He was firm, but he was a gentleman, and compassionate.

We were to take the boat across to Banika, he told us, and guard a storehouse for two weeks. We'd heard of Banika, but none of us had been there. Everything good came from Banika. The Navy had a supply dump on the island. If we got fresh meat, it came over from Banika. If we got fresh eggs, they were from Banika.

One of us asked what we'd be guarding. Beer and soda pop, Haldane told us. A whole warehouse. Thousands of cases. It was like sending foxes to guard the chicken coop.

I figured afterward that Captain Haldane and our first sergeant, Mo Darsey, had gone down a list and handpicked us for the assignment. I can't speak for myself, but everyone else chosen was a top-notch Marine. I felt proud to be in their company.

It didn't take us long to get to our warehouse on Banika, about a twenty-mile boat ride from Pavuvu. We had two six-man pyramid tents, on real wooden platforms for a change. The duty was light. Four hours on, ninety-six hours off. For chow, we went down to the wharf and climbed on board a ship that was anchored there. The first time I went aboard I almost fainted. I had never seen anything like that in the Pacific.

When we went in they sat us down and brought us menus. There were napkins and tablecloths on the tables. White linen towels to dry your face and hands. After we looked over the menu, the waiter asked, "What will you have, sir?" We could order anything—breakfast, lunch or dinner—and he'd bring it to us like we were in a restaurant. I'd never dreamed of being served like that anywhere in the Marines. On a troopship you'd just go through a line and they'd dish it out, just slop it on your tray.

We helped ourselves to a share from the warehouse. It was hot, but it was beer.

One Saturday night on Banika four of us were sitting around— Hillbilly Jones, Yarborough, myself, and somebody else. Maybe Sarrett. I can't recall. We were pouring 190-proof alcohol in the bottom of a canteen cup and filling the rest with grapefruit juice. We were singing and telling jokes and drinking that stuff, and by ten thirty we started to run low on grapefruit juice, and so we poured in more alcohol.

Oh, my God. You talk about drunk. I had to put all three of them to bed, I mean every single one. Haul him to his feet. There was a jeep outside that had a 250-gallon water tank on the back, with a spigot on the side. I'd wrestle each one out there and stick his head under the spigot and run water over him until I thought he could make it to the tent more or less upright. I'd get him there and put him on his cot. Tuck him in. All three of them.

And I was thinking, Man, I'm doing okay, you know? Here I've put these three drunks to bed and I'm still walking straight.

About three o'clock that morning I woke up vomiting. I want to tell you, I never vomited so hard in my life. I got up the next morning and looked over the side of my cot. And there was blood everywhere. I'd vomited so hard I'd vomited blood.

That was on Sunday morning. My first meal after that was on Thursday.

———

Toward the end of our stay on Pavuvu we had a visitor from Banika.

Bob Hope had been entertaining troops across the South Pacific. He had taken his whole USO troupe with him—singer Frances Langford, comedian Jerry Colonna, Tony Romano, who played the guitar. And a lively, pretty little blond dancer named Patty Thomas.

We weren't on their schedule. They'd been to Christmas Island, Tarawa, Kwajalein, Saipan, Bougainville, Tulagi. A Catalina flying boat that was taking them to Australia had made a crash-landing in a river bar, but they'd made it out okay. In late July they were putting on a show over on Banika.

Somebody had flown over and told Hope there was a whole division stuck on this little island, about to go into battle. We hadn't seen an outsider for months, much less a female outsider.

"Where are they?" he asked. Pavuvu, somebody told him.

Hope had never heard of it. "Where in the hell is that?" he asked.

We had no runway, but our one road could accommodate the occasional Piper Cub that flew in with messages or visiting officers. If the troupe could be ready the next morning, they could be flown over one by one.

We got word the same day and by next morning we had put up a makeshift stage down by the beach, at the end of an open area where we played baseball and drilled. By the time the first of the planes appeared, there must have been fifteen thousand of us standing in that field, all of us yelling our heads off. The pilot cut the engine on Jerry Colonna's plane as it circled over and we heard him let out that famous Colonna howl: "Yee . . . ow . . . ow." Even from the ground we could see his handlebar mustache and those shining white teeth.

The show lasted about ninety minutes, but it seemed shorter. Patty Thomas, who was wearing a skimpy skirt and a halter top, invited guys from the front rows to come up onstage and jitterbug with her. Hope and Colonna traded jokes.

Hope asked Colonna how he had enjoyed the flight from Banika.

"Tough sledding," Colonna said.

"Why tough sledding?" Hope asked.

"No snow."

We roared with laughter.

Somebody must have briefed them on Pavuvu, because Hope even got in a joke about our land crabs. He said they reminded him of Bing Crosby's racehorses—"they run sideways."

Pavuvu was so small, he said, "the gophers have to take turns coming up."

At the end of the show, Hope sang his theme song, "Thanks for the Memories." Then they got into their Piper Cubs and, one by one, took off. We stood alongside the road cheering.

For days afterward we'd talk about that show. It really lifted our spirits.

Years later, on one of his last television broadcasts, Hope called that appearance on Pavuvu one of the most moving shows he ever played.

"You knew when you walked out there that a lot of those guys you'd never see again," he said. "And as it worked out sixty percent of these kids were knocked off."

It was not quite as bad as that. But almost. Thirty percent of the First Division would be wounded or killed on Peleliu.

———

They passed around some maps and some fuzzy photographs taken from planes or through a submarine periscope. None of them showed any useful detail. It just looked like a lot of trees and some hills.

They'd also made a model. The island was even smaller than Pavuvu. We'd be landing across a wide beach stretching north to south. Two hundred yards beyond was the Jap airfield that was our first day's objective. Behind the airfield, mountains rose up and continued almost the whole length of the island. Except for the hills, they told us, most of the place was flat.

They didn't tell us the name yet.

Our training wrapped up with a couple big landing exercises. We didn't have our amtracs. They were still busy on Guam. So we used Higgins boats. They told us to come out of the amtracs ready for anything. Have bayonets fixed, a round chambered in our rifles and the safety on. Locked and loaded. Our ammo carriers were to have a couple mortar shells unfastened and ready to go.

They repeated over and over again the lesson learned on Guadalcanal:

"Get off the beach! Get your ass off the beach! Move in!"

Late on August 26, we filed on board LST 661. The next morning we were under way.

An LST was the largest ship the Navy could actually put right up on a beach. The hold would be full of amtracs and the amtracs would be full of troops. The big clamshell doors in the front of the ship would open and you'd just roll ashore. If there was a coral reef off the beach, the LST would stay farther out and the amtracs would rumble down the ramp into the water, form up and move to the beach in waves.

That's how it was supposed to work. Every now and then, we'd heard, an amtrac would go down the ramp, nose into the water, and sink. Just disappear.

The LST had a long deck for cargo. It could carry up to three hundred troops belowdecks and a couple dozen more in the forecastle, which was about two-thirds of the way back.

Our mortar section got lucky. The platoon leaders drew straws, and we were assigned to the troop quarters in the forecastle. Everyone else went belowdecks. All day long those steel sides and the deck soaked up that tropical sun, and all night they radiated the heat back into the compartments. Belowdecks was hot, cramped, stuffy. Pretty soon everyone was scrambling for any available place to sleep in and around the crates and equipment in the cargo area.

While we were at sea the division held landing rehearsals off Guadalcanal. Our amtracs and DUKWs had finally arrived, and they needed to practice launching them off the LSTs and getting them across a reef onto the beach. During one of these exercises, Major General William Rupertus, First Division's commander, slipped while boarding an amtrac. He fell back on the coral, breaking his ankle. His foot would be in a cast during the whole invasion.

When we arrived at Guadalcanal, other ships were pulling in from Banika, Tulagi, Espirito Santo. From all over the southwest Pacific it seemed. Some of the Old Breed, the Guadalcanal veterans, wanted to go ashore to see where they'd fought and visit the military cemetery.

We got a pep talk from one of them, First Sergeant Paul Bailey. He was soft-spoken, down to earth. A helluva good Marine. He'd joined us on Pavuvu.

He told us for the first time where we were going—Peleliu. He said it wouldn't be easy, that a lot of us wouldn't be coming back. But we were going in and we were going to take it as quickly as possible with as few casualties as possible.

"Don't be dumb," Sergeant Bailey said. "We want to go in there and play it smart." The faster we killed Japs, the sooner we'd get off that island.

I don't know if those pep talks they always gave us before a battle helped or hindered. Those of us who had been through it already knew a lot of us weren't coming back, that a lot of us would be killed, a lot would be wounded or maimed for the rest of our lives.

We knew any time you go into combat, it's not pretty.

On September 4, we filed back on board LST 661 and weighed anchor. There were more than sixteen thousand of us, aboard thirty LSTs and a handful of troop transports. LSTs are slow, about seven knots. So we got a head start. The faster transport ships sailed four days later and gradually caught up with us. We headed northwest through the Solomon Islands, then along the east coast of New Guinea toward the equator. We passed through a couple rain squalls, but otherwise we were on a calm, beautiful sea. We sat on the deck cleaning and recleaning salt corrosion off our weapons. We took our ammo out of the clips, polished it and reloaded. We sharpened our KA-BARS, packed and re-packed our gear. Sometimes the Navy would throw a couple barrels overboard and their gunners would practice shooting at them.

Afternoons some of us gathered around Hillbilly Jones. We sang "Red River Valley" or some other favorite.

From this valley they say you are going,
I will miss your bright eyes and sweet smile . . .

I liked to stand at the railing and watch the porpoises play in the wake of the ship, the flying fish glide over the crests of the waves. Off on the horizon I could see dozens of other ships. Aircraft carriers. Battleships. We had the *Pennsylvania, Idaho, Maryland, Mississippi,* and *Tennessee* with us. And smaller ships. Cruisers, I assumed. Closer in, destroyers and PT boats were escorting us. We were all zigzagging as we sailed along, changing direction every fifteen minutes or so. One afternoon the sirens sounded, a signal that there was a sub somewhere around us. The PT boats circled trying to locate him. They dropped some depth charges. I don't know if they found him, but we got by without any of our ships being damaged.

I always loved those PT boats, ever since I saw them at Talasea. They were the Corsair fighter planes of the sea, sleek and agile. They were something else.

I read years later that somewhere along the way sealed envelopes

The day after Christmas 1943, on Cape Gloucester Peninsula, New Britain. This, to me, is the ultimate picture of the combat Marine. Look at his torn pants. His elbow is probably out, too. He's smoking one of those cheap cigarettes they gave us and he's got that thousand-yard stare. He knows what he's walking into, and he knows that it's not going to be pretty.

Landing at Cape Gloucester, December 26, 1943. The shallow-draft LCIs can move in where water is only waist-deep. We'd stay wet for the next four months on that damned island.

The important thing was to keep your rifle high and dry in the troubled waters at Cape Gloucester. "Feather Merchants"—the shorties in the outfit—could find themselves in a heap of trouble, with waves up to their armpits. At six feet plus, I did okay, though. December 26, 1943.

Another wet-ass picture on Cape Gloucester. Even if we got a day with no rain, there were always streams to be crossed. If they were too wide or too deep or too swift to ford, we followed them down to the beach and crossed on a sandbar.

Courtesy of the National Archives

When comedian Bob Hope heard we were stuck on Pavuvu, getting ready for Peleliu, he insisted on putting on a show for us. Here, Hope and First Lieutenant Robert W. Bechers, the general's aide, stand next to the Piper Cub that brought Hope's USO troupe to Pavuvu. It took that little grasshopper several trips to ferry everybody across from Banika and several trips to get them back. Note the First Marine Division insignia on the fuselage. August 7, 1944, Pavuvu, Russell Islands.

Courtesy of the National Archives

Jerry Colona and his sidekick, Tony Romano, clown around onstage in front of a sea of smiling Marines on Pavuvu. I'm about a fourth of the way back in that crowd. It was a terrific show, and for a few hours, it took our minds off what was coming.

September 15, 1944. We're hitting the beach at Peleliu. The Japanese air base that is our first day's objective is just beyond the sand. And beyond the air base are Bloody Nose Ridge, the Umurbrogol Mountains, and almost two months of the bloodiest combat in the Pacific war.

Holding our front-line position onPeleliu, first day. There's always someone looking back, because you never knew when the Japs were going to come creeping out of caves and pillboxes behind us. I don't remember any photographers taking our picture, but I was kind of preoccupied.

Riflemen hunkered down behind a tank on Peleliu and directing their fire toward something—probably a pillbox or a cave—in the higher ground to the right.

Two Marines on Peleliu ease up on a Japanese pillbox scraped out of hard coral rock. The occupants, still alive when this photo was taken, have set up a machine gun in there and are not coming out, leaving the Marines to clean them out with phosphorous grenades, a satchel charge, or a flamethrower.

There were more than five hundred of these pillboxes on Peleliu, and each had to be cleaned out by hard-fighting Marines. Most were impossible to see until you'd nearly stumbled over them.

The strafing and shelling have let up and Marines cross the beach and head for the tiny landing strip during our textbook assault on Ngesebus, the small island just north of Peleliu, September 28, 1944. After the awful slaughter on the main island, we got in here pretty easy with just a little sniper fire. The whole thing was over in two days.

A flamethrower specialist and his assistant wait on Ngesebus beach. That backpack weighs seventy pounds, so you had to be big to carry a flamethrower. The assistant operates the valve on the back of the pack and provides protection, usually with a tommy gun.

Courtesy of the National Archives

Riflemen advance across Ngesebus behind an amtrac. Pretty close to here our mortar section encountered a supposedly unoccupied Jap bunker, which held up our advance until another amtrac, mounting a .75, and a flamethrower helped us clean it out.

Courtesy of the National Archives

Back on Peleliu a Marine with a BAR fires on Jap positions. The man behind him wields an M1. Barely visible to their left in the blasted landscape of rock and tree limbs is the body of an enemy soldier.

The enemy is just across the ridge, and a Marine is firing rifle grenades in an effort to dig them out. This was a pretty effective weapon, like a small mortar but with no sight, so you had to fire several rounds to get on-target.

A Corsair of the Second Marine Aircraft Wing is just pulling up from his napalm run on Japs holed up in one of the Five Sisters, and is swinging around to return to the Peleliu air base, a scant 1,500 yards away. The whole operation, takeoff to landing, took a few minutes, not enough time to retract the landing gear. I've heard this was the shortest bombing run in World War II.

Courtesy of the National Archives

Coming in to Okinawa, everything was black smoke and the flash and deafening roar of the big guns on the Navy's battleships. Despite one of the largest invasion fleets ever assembled, we encountered very little opposition going ashore. One of a few Jap snipers—put there mainly to aggravate us, I think—managed to hit Colonel John Gustafson in the arm as he stepped off an amtrac. He reboarded and was taken back to the ship.

Courtesy of the National Archives

Private Holbrack of Kansas City, Kansas, fires a BAR at a group of Japs who have been caught in the open changing positions, May 2, 1945, on Okinawa. I shot expert on the lighter M1, but the BAR had a V-shaped sight that I was never able to get used to. One officer suspected I just didn't want to carry around the extra weight.

Courtesy of the National Archives

Stripped of his clothing by a Japanese mortar shell, shocked, and in pain, a Marine is still able to hobble to the rear of the lines with the help of a buddy. Elsewhere on May 8, 1945, the Allies are celebrating V-E day, victory in Europe. But here in Okinawa it's still combat as usual.

Courtesy of the National Archives

K Company, Third Battalion is moving the front line forward across Okinawa, from ridge to valley to ridge to valley. They all had names but I could never remember them. Still can't.

Courtesy of the National Archives

A Marine dashes for cover through Jap machine-gun fire in one place a lot of us remembered by name. In the eight days it took to cross the draw later known as "Death Valley," Marines took more than 125 casualties. May 10, 1945, Okinawa.

Courtesy of the National Archives

With little more than sticks to hide behind, a BAR man fires on a Jap machine-gun nest on Wana Ridge, where I was wounded on May 20.

A First Division Marine fires a tommy submachine gun during the assault on Wana Ridge. The ridge was key to securing the fortress at Shuri Castle, where the main Japanese headquarters occupied an extensive tunnel system.

Nine Marines give their undivided attention to an Okinawan cave entrance, oozing smoke after detonation of a satchel charge. Any surviving Jap who tries to dash to safety faces a brief and brutal reception. The cave, near the city of Naha, is one of hundreds occupied by Japs in a last-gasp defense of the island.

Courtesy of the National Archives

In the final weeks of combat on Okinawa, four litter bearers rush a Marine wounded by a Jap sniper to medical treatment. Usually drawn from among cooks, musicians, and other noncombat Marines, litter bearers again and again put themselves in harm's way to carry a fellow Marine to safety.

Courtesy of the National Archives

Oh, yeah! I learned to love those Marine Corsairs. Loosing their loads of rockets against Japanese positions, the sleek fighter planes with the bent wings became a familiar sight and saved our bacon many times on Okinawa.

My parents, Joseph Harmon Burgin and Beulah May Perry Burgin, drove 106 miles from Jewett to Dallas to stand beside their proud son when he was awarded the Bronze Star for eliminating an enemy machine-gun nest on Okinawa. I'm wearing my first and only set of dress blues, purchased for the occasion.

Romus Valton Burgin in 1946.

Still waiting for the papers to clear so she can come to the U.S. and marry her Marine, Florence Riseley sits for the camera in Melbourne.

Courtesy of R. V. Burgin

Courtesy of R. V. Burgin

Florence thought we'd be married in two weeks, on her twenty-first birthday, when she stepped off the train in Dallas on January 27, 1947. But only two days have passed, and here we are standing at the altar at Saner Avenue Church of Christ. That's my sister Imogene on the left, and my old Marine buddy Clyde "Tex" Cummings, on the right. The flower girls are my niece Jodie Minkler (*right*) and Sue Weimer, daughter of a friend.

A photo of me in my dress blues, wearing my Bronze Star. On the left is my Bronze Star, with my Rifle Expert Badge below it. On the right, my Purple Heart and my Pistol Sharpshooter badge.

To this day, I've never forgotten my time in the Pacific. This is my wall of memories in my home, complete with the K Company photo from Peleliu, my Bronze Star, and my KA-BAR knife.

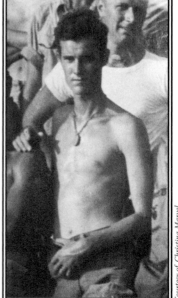

That's me the day before we left Peleliu, exhausted after weeks of hard fighting.

were passed out to all the unit commanders and to the war correspondents that accompanied the fleet. The envelopes were not to be opened until September 14, the day before the invasion.

Inside was a message from General Rupertus. He predicted the battle for Peleliu would be rough but short. "A quickie," he wrote. In and out in three days. Maybe in two.

Almost all the correspondents decided then and there that the invasion of Peleliu would not be worth their time. Most of them decided to stay with the ships and eventually move on to something more newsworthy.

I am convinced that's why Peleliu never got the attention it deserves. The big battles that everyone's heard of—Iwo Jima, Guadalcanal—they were highly publicized. But Peleliu, nobody's ever heard of that.

We sailed twenty-one hundred miles in eleven days. Sometime after midnight September 14, I could feel the ship slow, then stop. As usual, I was up early—always the country boy. In the darkness I felt around for the ankle-high combat shoes we called boondockers, pulled them on and laced them up. I sat there for a few minutes. Then Johnny Marmet came in.

"Okay, Burgin. Let's get 'em up."

We yelled for everyone to hit the deck. In minutes there were men dressing, shaving, waiting for the toilets. We could already smell the steak and eggs from the galley, the traditional Marine Corps breakfast before battle. Some of us could eat, some of us couldn't.

Private Vincent Santos could.

"When's the last time you got steak and eggs?" he asked. "And when's the next time you're going to get steak and eggs? So I'm making the best of it."

Santos would lose his steak and eggs on the amtrac.

After breakfast we lined up for the head and then stumbled out onto the deck. The brightest stars still hung in the sky. There was already a soft glow in the east.

About then one of those little Piper Cub–type spotter planes came buzzing along, maybe eight hundred to a thousand yards in front of us and just above the water. One of the forward antiaircraft guns barked, opening fire on him. Tracers went arcing into the darkness.

Everybody started yelling, "You damned idiot! That's one of ours!"

The plane dodged and wobbled off, not hit, thank goodness.

Just as the sun showed above the horizon, all hell broke loose. Every gun in the Navy started in at once. The sea lit up like flashbulbs. Thunder rolled across the waves and rumbled back at us. A few minutes later the first planes from the carriers flew over, headed north, Hellcat fighters and Dauntless dive-bombers loaded with napalm and five-hundred-pound bombs. We could see pink and orange splashes in the distance and a few seconds later hear the *thump-thump* of the explosions.

In the growing light, smoke spread out into a long, low smudge across the northern horizon, east to west. It was the only cloud in the sky that morning. The bombardment let up long enough for the planes to get in, then picked up again.

The ship's bell rang, and we got the order to stand by.

We helped one another with our packs and gear, snubbing up straps and making sure everything was secure. M1s and carbines slung over our left shoulders, we stood at the ladders leading down to the tank deck where the amtracs were waiting for us.

I just mumbled, "God, I'm in your hands. Take care of me." That was always my prayer. I kept it short. I didn't want to burden Him. He had other people to look after.

CHAPTER 5

The Unnecessary Island

You read nowadays that the Battle of Peleliu should never have been fought. We should never have invaded, experts say. And I agree.

We took that island to secure the airfield so the Japs couldn't use it against MacArthur when he was landing on Mindanao, to the west. But we had already bombed that airfield three months before, and we could have gone on bombing it 24-7. We could have made it absolutely unusable. There was no way the Japs could have rebuilt it in time. They were finished as an air power.

Just days before our landing at Peleliu, Admiral Bull Halsey wanted to pull out, but Admiral Nimitz, his superior, refused. General MacArthur wanted to take the island as well, and President Roosevelt approved it. We were committed.

Those of us on the ground didn't know anything about all that. Good idea or bad idea, we didn't have time to dwell on it. The First Marines under Colonel Lewis Puller—nicknamed Chesty—were fighting for their lives on the Point, a hump of coral rock on the northwestern tip of the island. We were lost in the forest east of the airfield, no idea where we were. Every one of us was fighting for his life. We talked about it a lot after the fact. But not while we were there. We were pretty well occupied.

Peleliu would keep us busier than anybody ever imagined. General Rupertus was off the mark when he said we'd be in and out in two or three days. The maps and photographs and the model we'd all studied so carefully didn't tell the whole story. They didn't tell us that a lot of that level ground was thick mangrove swamp. They didn't tell us that beneath the tops of the trees the ridges were steep, and honeycombed with more than five hundred limestone caves and man-made tunnels. One of them was big enough to hide fifteen hundred troops. They didn't tell us that before it was over we'd have to fight our way from one cave to the next. One of our generals said it was like fighting in Swiss cheese.

The Japs had been on Peleliu since they seized it from the Germans during World War I. They'd had plenty of time to dig in. Starting in the 1930s they'd put the natives to work and brought in hundreds of

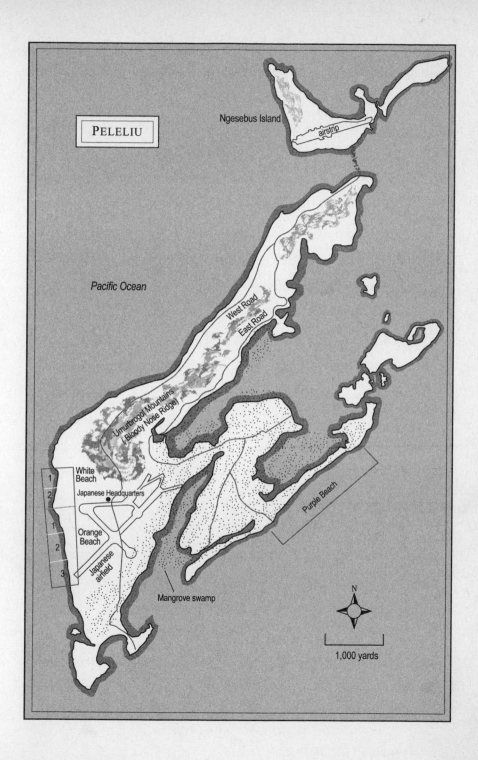

PELELIU

Ngesebus Island

airstrip

Pacific Ocean

West Road

East Road

Umurbrogol Mountains
(Bloody Nose Ridge)

White
Beach

1

2

Japanese Headquarters

1

Orange
Beach

2

Japanese
airfield

3

Purple Beach

Mangrove swamp

N

1,000 yards

Korean tunnel diggers, enlarging the caves and connecting them until the whole place was like a termite nest.

The island was coral rock, shaped like a crab claw with two prongs, a larger and a smaller, pointing northeast. A series of parallel ridges ran up the bigger prong of the claw. Roads skirted either side of the ridges and joined at the north end of the island, where the Japs had a phosphate mine. From there, a five-hundred-foot causeway led to a smaller island, Ngesebus. Ngesebus was mostly flat, and the Japs had started building a smaller airfield there. We'd have to take care of that sooner or later.

Peleliu was just north of the equator. We didn't think about just how hot and dry it would get until we got there. We had no idea how sharp that coral was, how it could shred your clothes and boondockers and tear your skin. How even a minor wound would fester and seem to take weeks to heal.

With all the other things we were to face the first couple of days, the most aggravating was thirst. Most of us had come ashore with two full canteens. By the time K Company dug in that first night, lost somewhere in the scrub and out of touch with the rest of our units, we could shake our canteens and hear the last few drops slosh around. The daytime temperature had been well over a hundred degrees. We'd been gulping water like we had an endless supply.

I didn't know where the information was coming from, but we were hearing that it had been a bad day for the whole First Division. We had lost more than a thousand men wounded or killed. It's probably a good thing we didn't know just how bad the situation was, or that the First Regiment was fighting for their lives, barely clinging to the Point. We knew our battalion commander was out of action, either wounded or killed, and that his executive officer was dead. We didn't know who was running things.

Just before midnight we found out.

We were expecting Jap infiltrators when two figures walked out of the brush and gave the password. It was Lieutenant Colonel Lewis Walt, our battalion commander on New Britain, and his runner. After Shofner had been taken out to a hospital ship, Walt, who was now the Fifth Regiment's executive officer, had taken charge of Third Battalion. With communications still down, he set out in the darkness to find his scattered companies and put them back into some kind of order. He'd already rounded up I and L companies. When he found us he led us back toward the airfield and positioned us facing south just behind Second Battalion, which was facing north. We'd be watching one another's backs through the rest of the night.

We dug mortar emplacements, registered the two guns with a couple test rounds, laid out our KA-BARS where they'd be handy, and settled in for a long, restless night.

The water situation hadn't improved, and by dawn there were a lot of empty canteens. The coral never cooled during all the time we were on Peleliu. Even at night it stayed warm, and the morning sun soon turned it into a griddle. Some of our guys went searching and found a cistern at the edge of the airstrip with a little pool of stagnant water about ten or twelve feet down. Word spread and guys started to gather around, passing their canteens down to be filled. We were an excellent target. The water didn't look too good to me, silty and probably polluted. But none of us were picky at that point. Before long they managed to bring up a couple of the fifty-gallon drums from the beach, old diesel containers that were supposed to have been steam-cleaned on Pavuvu before they were filled with water. We lined up to fill our canteens, but it was even worse than the water from the cistern, tea-colored and smelling strongly of fuel oil. Guys would take a mouthful and spit it out. Those that swallowed it would throw up a few minutes later. Some of them had the dry heaves all morning.

I thought, If anyone lights a match around us we'll all be turned into human flamethrowers.

About this time the Japs opened up on us from the high ground overlooking the airfield. We called it Bloody Nose Ridge, and it bloodied us good. They could see us in the morning light, but we couldn't see them. The Navy's guns and our own heavy artillery on the beach answered, but I don't think we had much effect. The Japs were shooting from the mouths of caves a couple hundred feet up, where we couldn't get at them. They'd wheel a gun to the entrance, fire, and wheel it back out of sight.

As the enemy poured steel down on us, we got the word to prepare to move out. The whole Fifth Regiment was to attack straight across the airfield, then swing north. We'd be on the right, moving across the southern end. Second Battalion was on our left. They'd take the middle. Then on their left, First Battalion, which had hooked up with elements of the First Marines' Second Battalion. Off on our right in the scrub jungle were the Seventh Marines.

We'd practiced the drill on Pavuvu. Stay down until the signal. Keep a distance between one another so we present a scattered target. Move fast and don't stop until we get to the far side. A moving target is harder to hit. We crouched in the underbrush, listening to the guns bang away at one another. Then the word came: "Move out!"

That was the longest walk I ever took in my life. We were on the go. We were moving, bent over at a trot. Everything was coming at us— mortars, artillery, machine-gun and rifle fire. You heard the hiss and zing of shrapnel and bullets all around you. We were as exposed as bugs on a breakfast table. I kept yelling, "Keep moving! Keep moving!"

The field was littered with scraps from the tank battle the day before, empty ammo boxes, chunks of shrapnel bouncing and skittering along. There were a couple wrecked Jap warplanes, including one of their twin-engine "Betty" bombers.

I saw Merriel "Snafu" Shelton go down, carrying the mortar tube. Sledgehammer went down right behind him, cradling a bag of mortar shells in his arms. Neither was hit and both got up and started off again.

We couldn't fire back at our tormentors because we were on the run. We didn't want to expose ourselves any longer than we had to. But it was frustrating. After what seemed like ages, a line of brush appeared in front of us. We dove into the shade, panting and sweating. For the first time I realized how hot we had been coming across. It was like the Japs had one more weapon on their side, the sun.

Everyone was accounted for. Mortar section hadn't lost a man in the mad dash. But K Company lost two dead and five wounded. One of them was Private First Class Robert Oswalt, shot through the head. He was the one I had almost shot between the eyes myself on New Britain when he came crawling out of his foxhole at night begging for a drink of water. Suddenly I felt awful.

Once we were across the airfield, our orders were to swing north and head for the low area east of Bloody Nose Ridge, near the coast. There we'd link up with the Second Battalion. As we started north we found our battalion getting squeezed between the Second Battalion and the Seventh Marines, who were still clearing out the swamps.

At the north edge of the field, a few yards on our left, we passed a two-story concrete shell, evidently the air base headquarters. By the time we saw it, one of the battleships had blasted it with fourteen-inch guns, but the walls were at least a foot thick with steel reinforcing, and it was still standing. Some other Marine unit had dislodged the Japs there and moved in.

Beyond the northeast corner of the airfield, we found ourselves in dense scrub again. Beyond lay a patch of swamp with the sea shimmering in the distance. The main road running north along the east side of the island cut through here, but we stayed out of sight. We found a clear space where we could set up the mortars and pound in the aiming stakes to orient the weapons. Late in the afternoon we fired a few rounds to register the guns and scraped out foxholes in the hard coral, piling up rocks and logs around them. All the time we kept our eyes on the wall of scrub around us, expecting a banzai attack any minute. It never came. In fact, the Japs never charged us banzai-style on Peleliu like they had on New Britain. They knew better. Now they waited until dark. Then they came creeping out of their caves to slit our throats.

As it happened, our second night passed quietly. Orders for the next day were to continue to advance north and relieve First Battalion. They had been playing a cat-and-mouse game with the Japs all afternoon, working their way along the lower slopes of the ridge. Whenever they moved forward, Jap mortars and artillery shells would come pouring down on them from the hills. Whenever they stopped, the fire stopped.

Next morning we set out for our rendezvous with First Battalion, still picking our way through dense scrub. I could tell it was going to be a hot one. As the sun climbed higher guys started dropping out with heat prostration, and we had to stop more and more frequently. We were burning through our salt tablets.

The east flank of Bloody Nose Ridge rose up on our right, and as we advanced we started coming under vicious artillery and mortar fire from the heights. We couldn't use our own mortars for fear of dropping them on First Battalion, which was somewhere between us and the ridge. By noon we had linked up with them and we took their place in the front lines. When we started forward again we almost immediately ran into a wall of fire that kept pinning us down all afternoon. When we tried to move forward, the Japs would open up on us. There's no feeling on earth as vulnerable as having somebody fire shells down on you from up above.

Second Battalion had pulled to our right and was making better progress through the mangroves. Behind them somewhere was the Seventh Marines. Our company finally found our own little patch of mangroves and pushed through until we came out in a coconut grove and, on the far side, an open area. This had once been a native village, but the Japs had taken over and built rows of barracks. During the landing we had bombed and shelled the area pretty thoroughly, and there wasn't much left but piles of charred lumber.

Our supplies caught up with us by late afternoon, including some precious water. Things seemed about to take a turn for the better.

The next morning Second Battalion was ordered east across a narrow neck of land that joined the larger of Peleliu's crab claws to the smaller. Japs had been spotted in that area. The Marines had just started across when a group of Navy fighters came roaring over, strafing the column from one end to the other. This mistake cost the Corps almost three dozen men. Our battalion was hurried forward to reinforce them. We were coming up on the same neck of land, following a crude road with swamp on either side of us, when shells—*big* shells—started raining down on us. I knew they were ours because they were screaming right over our backs and crashing just in front, showering us with mud and coral rock. We could feel the thump of the concussions on our dungarees before we all hit the ground.

We'd been stringing out communication wire as we went. I grabbed the sound-powered phone to the command post.

"We're taking fire from behind us up here!" I shouted.

"No, that can't be ours!"

"Don't by God tell me it's not ours! It's coming from the damned airfield, and we've *got* the airfield. I'm telling you what the hell it is! It's our damned artillery and it's a 155. I'm looking at it as it lands. Get word back to them to cut it out. They're too damned close."

That was the first time I ever experienced an airburst. Those things are wicked. The shell comes in and explodes before it hits the ground, and the shrapnel slices down through anything that isn't under cover. A foxhole or a trench—it doesn't make a damn bit of difference where you're at. There's no place to hide from an airburst. I thought for sure that stuff was going to eat us up. But by some miracle, nobody was hit.

After the artillery let up we moved on. By early afternoon we dug in south of the Second Battalion.

The Japs had their main base up on Babelthuap, a larger island about forty miles north of Peleliu. Our intelligence had information that they might send a force across to relieve their Peleliu garrison and drive us off the island. It wasn't clear to us what a couple hundred Marines could do to stop a major landing, but at least we could sound the alarm and hold them off for a while. As we pushed through the swamps on the smaller claw we ran into an occasional sniper. But the next day or two was about the quietest we were to experience on Peleliu.

The third day they sent about forty of us on an extended patrol down to the tip of a long, narrow peninsula running along the southeast coast of the island. Hillbilly Jones was in charge and we had an Army man with a war dog, a big Doberman that could smell the Japs.

There were a couple of islands off the tip, and we were told about two thousand Japs were hidden there. When the tide went out it would be easy for them to wade across, come up the peninsula and catch us by surprise. We were supposed to set up and watch for them.

It was a spooky place to start with, gloomy and dark, with dense trees and thick vines snaking all over the place and tangles of roots that looked like the legs of some giant spider. Sledge was goggling at the birds, and I had to remind him to keep his mind on business. We settled near an abandoned Jap bunker, where Hillbilly set up his command post. The rest of us spread out and dug in. For a change the ground was soft enough to dig real foxholes. We set up our gun at the water's edge and pointed it where we thought they'd try to cross. We didn't dare fire a register round because every sound would carry right across the water. In fact, we were ordered to stay quiet, not light up a smoke, not advertise our presence in any way.

The sun went down, leaving us to our rations and to the mosquitoes. Sergeant Elmo Haney, who'd amused us with his antics on Pavuvu, had come along. He was more Asiatic than usual that night. He kept moving up and down the line urging everyone in a hoarse whisper to check their weapons, lock and load, stay alert. The Japs might come across at any minute with fixed bayonets, he warned. He disappeared, but pretty soon he was back again to see if we knew the password. Check your weapons. Stay alert. He was starting to get to us.

Fact is, we were more than alert. We were forty twitching bundles of nerves. We jumped at every sound. A fish splashing out in the water, some animal snapping a twig or some bird ruffling its feathers— anything could set us off. Nobody was getting any sleep.

I was near the command post around midnight when we all heard someone start to moan. "Ooooooooooh. Oooooooooh. Dog! They're gonna kill me, dog! Help me! Oooooooooooooh!" It was the dog handler. He went on and on, getting louder, like some siren. Somebody shushed him, then somebody tackled him in the darkness. I could hear them thrashing around, grunts and moans.

"Quiet that man!" Hillbilly ordered. Someone else called for our corpsman.

The dog handler was screaming louder. "Help me. Oh, dog! God! Help me! Help me!"

"Shut that man up!" Hillbilly hissed.

Several of us were wrestling him now, while the corpsman got out his syringe. He gave him a shot of morphine, but it just seemed to egg him on. He howled louder, calling on his dog, or God, to save him.

"The Japs have got me! The Japs have got me! Save me, dog!"

The corpsman gave him another shot, enough morphine by now to kill a horse. Anything to shut him up. He went on yelling, kicking and punching at anyone who came near. If the Japs couldn't hear him, we were sure they were deaf.

Hillbilly was trying to talk him down in low, soothing tones. "It's okay, son. You're going to be okay."

He kept yelling.

Someone said, "Hit him! Shut him the hell up!" And someone else grabbed an entrenching tool and swung.

We heard a sharp *whang!*, and then silence.

We sat there for a long time, nobody talking. To tell the truth, we were more rattled than if the Japs had come.

Hillbilly got on the phone to battalion headquarters. Major John Gustafson had taken over from Colonel Walt as commander.

"John, we need to come out of here," Hillbilly said.

We couldn't hear the other side of the conversation.

"No, John. I'm telling you, we need to come out of here. We've had a situation here and everybody's nerves are shot. We need to get the hell out."

By daybreak a tank found its way to us through the jungle. We'd covered the body of the dog handler with his poncho and loaded it on the tank and started back, through the dripping trees.

Later we learned two barges full of Japs tried to land farther north that night and the night after. A Navy ship intercepted them and sank both vessels. But no Japs crossed over where we had been watching.

It was another one of those nights we didn't talk about afterward. None of us was proud of it, but that dog handler had endangered all of us, the whole crew that was there in the jungle. We'd done what we had to do. I was as close as anybody to what happened, three or four feet away. I'd seen who'd swung the shovel. I knew who did it. He did something that needed to be done. As long as any of us is alive, none of us will reveal who it was.

The strange thing is that the Doberman was silent during the whole deal.

We continued our patrols for a couple of days until the smaller claw was declared secure. K Company dug in along the shore near an area that had been designated Purple Beach, where we'd been expecting a Jap landing. We had fared pretty well so far compared to other units. We lost thirty-seven men, killed or wounded. The mortar section hadn't lost anybody.

But on the opposite side of Peleliu the First Marines were in terrible shape. After the bitter down-to-the-last-man fight for the Point, Chesty Puller had pushed them on to fight for the high ground beyond the airfield. Bloody Nose Ridge was just the start of it. Behind that and continuing halfway up the island was a series of steep-sided coral ridges, the tallest about five hundred feet, with narrow canyons between. These were the Umurbrogol Mountains. The photographs had shown only a thick carpet of trees. Even after we'd bombed and napalmed most of the cover, you couldn't make sense of the terrain. The slopes tilted every which way and they were shot through with cracks, crevices, caves and tunnels where the Japs were dug in and waiting. This was our nightmare for the rest of the time we fought on Peleliu, and long after we'd left.

The First Marines' Third Battalion was on the west side, the coastal flats. But their First and Second battalions had tackled the Umurbrogols head-on. No sooner had they fought to the top of one ridge than the Japs on the ridge behind had thrown them back. It was cave-to-cave fighting. There was no way they could dig them out. They'd seal up one entrance with a satchel charge and the Japs would fire at them from two other entrances. There wasn't anything you could call a front line, like we'd had on New Britain and we'd have on Okinawa. It was a different kind of warfare.

Out in the mangrove jungle, we'd escaped the worst of it. But we'd get our own taste soon enough.

After a week fighting on the Point and then on the ridges, there was hardly anything left of the First Marines. Puller was ordered to pull the First Regiment back. Over the protests of General Rupertus, who wanted Peleliu to be an all-Marine show, the Army's 321st Regimental Combat Team was brought in. They'd just come off a brief but successful fight for Angaur, a small island about six miles south of Peleliu.

This was the start of a whole different approach to the fight for the Umurbrogols, and the Fifth Marines were going to play our part.

About September 25, elements of the First Marines started settling in our area out on the smaller claw, waiting for a ship to take them back to Pavuvu for a well-earned rest. We got an order to withdraw to the east road, where trucks would be waiting for us. We gathered all our gear and started back the way we'd come. Somewhere near the neck where we'd taken friendly fire, we were marching along single file on the side of the road when we met the raggedest bunch of Marines I'd ever seen, coming our direction along the other side of the road. They were all that was left of Puller's First Regiment. We stopped and swapped news. We found out they had lost about three-quarters of their regiment. What was left looked like ghosts of Marines. They went their way and we went ours, wondering what we were getting into.

The trucks were waiting. We slung our gear aboard, climbed on and headed south, back toward the airfield. Things had changed. We no longer came under sustained fire from the ridge. The trucks turned west across the northern edge of the field, and we got a look at what had been going on since we had crossed it the week before.

The Seabees had arrived and gone to work. Bulldozers and graders were all over the place, and a cloud of fine coral dust hung over the scene. The carcasses of Jap planes had been dragged off the field and the pockmarked runways had been filled in and smoothed out. Little spotter planes were flitting around. As frogmen had blasted passages through the reef so the LSTs could come ashore, the grasshoppers had arrived on the beach in crates. Crews had put them together in a day or two, and now they were spotting for artillery. A group of stubby Hellcat fighters had flown in and taken up residence, even though the edge of the field was still within range of Jap mortars. The Seabees and aircrews were living in neat rows of tents, and they'd set up a mess hall. It was downright luxurious.

We went our dusty, bouncing way to the west road and turned north. The farther we rode, the closer the shore came in on our left and the rugged ridges of the Umurbrogols on our right. We'd gone just a short distance before we started seeing dogfaces, Army troops from the 321st. The trucks stopped and let us out. We exchanged scuttlebutt with the soldiers, who were going to stay behind while we moved through them. The road already had a reputation. They were calling it Sniper's Alley.

We waited an hour or two for a couple Sherman tanks and then started north. We were close enough to the ocean to hear waves slapping the rocks along the shore. Trees closed in on our right, and as the afternoon wore on the shadows of the ridge started to fall across the road. Corporal John Teskevich and several of our riflemen had climbed on board and were riding along when a Jap sniper that nobody ever saw shot Teskevich through the stomach. I was maybe fifty yards away. He died on the spot.

Teskevich was a good Marine. A tough, scrappy coal miner from Pennsylvania with a head of thick black hair and a big handlebar mustache that was his pride and joy, he had been one of our crew that Captain Haldane sent over to guard the beer storehouse on Banika. One morning while he was still sleeping, someone snuck into his tent and shaved off half of his mustache. Teskevich came roaring out, yelling that he'd fight the whole bunch of us. He looked pretty comical with half a mustache. Sergeant Jim Day got him calmed down, but I really do believe he would have taken us all on at once. I don't know who did that, probably never will know.

Occasional sniper fire continued as we moved on, but nobody else was hit. When we stopped for the evening word was passed along to watch for infiltrators. Our line extended from the road to the shoreline, no more than 150 feet to our left. We were under the eyes of the Japs up in the caves on the ridge, and we knew there were more scattered through the woods to the right of the road. But Captain Haldane thought the Japs might try to wade along the shore and come in on our left. Jim Burke and I scraped out foxholes a few feet apart where we had a clear view of the water. Again it was impossible to dig deep in the hard coral, so we piled up rocks around our positions and waited. Just before dark, Captain Haldane ordered artillery to work over the woods in front of us along the base of the ridge. It was satisfying to hear those incoming 75s. We'd soon find out if they did much good.

A little after dark, Jim whispered that he heard someone splashing out in the water. A low-hanging half-moon cast a long bar of light across the waves. We watched and waited, and pretty soon we heard voices from that direction. I never could figure out why the Japs would jabber when they were trying to sneak around in the dark. But they always did.

Jim saw him first, a silhouette moving along in the moonlight just offshore. He said later all he really saw at first was the head and shoulders.

"Burgin, give me your rifle," he whispered. He had been carrying only his .45. "I can see that son of a bitch."

I eased my M1 over to him. I heard the safety softly click.

We waited for five or ten seconds. Then Jim fired and there was a splash.

"Got him," I said.

Jim handed my rifle back. "Thank you very much," he said.

Then he shouted, "Heads up, you guys. There's more of them out there."

Up closer to the road Sledgehammer and Snafu Shelton were sharing a foxhole. The drill was that one man would sleep while the other kept watch. An hour on, an hour off.

Sledge was on watch a few hours before dawn. Snafu was sleeping, snoring as usual and occasionally muttering to himself. Probably something like "We need more men in here!" That was his constant complaint no matter where we were.

In the moonlight, the coral road was a bright ribbon through the dark wall of trees. While Sledge watched, two figures popped out of the darkness on the other side of the road, yelling something in Japanese and waving their arms. One of them cut to Sledge's right, ran down the road and disappeared to where Sledge knew another company was dug in.

The other figure ran straight for Sledge, waving a bayonet over his head.

Sledge grabbed his carbine, but hesitated. Other Marines lay in his line of fire.

With a yell, the oncoming Jap disappeared into a nearer foxhole. There was a series of thuds and grunts and yells, the sounds of a wild struggle. Then as Sledge watched, a figure jumped out of the hole and started in the direction of the command post nearby. Just then a Marine stood up and swung his rifle by the barrel, clubbing the running figure and bringing him down in midstride.

Down the road, where the first Jap had disappeared, someone started screaming wildly—Jap or Marine, Sledge couldn't tell. Then the screaming stopped. The figure clubbed with the rifle lay in the road groaning.

There was a rifle shot from the foxhole just in front of Sledge, and someone yelled, "I got him."

Everyone was awake now, but nobody knew what had happened.

"How many were there?" somebody asked.

"I saw two," Sledge said.

"There must have been more," somebody else said.

No, Sledge insisted. Two. One ran across the road and the other ran down to the right, where he got shot.

Then who was that groaning in the road? the other Marine asked.

"I don't know," Sledge said. "I didn't see but two of them. I'm sure of it."

"I'll check it out," somebody said and crawled out onto the road in the direction the groans were coming from. There was a sharp report of a .45, and the Marine crawled back to his foxhole.

In the graying light before dawn, Sledge looked over at the figure lying in the road. Somehow it didn't look Jap. He wore Marine leggings. Sledge crawled over for a closer look.

He recognized the fallen man instantly. It was Bill Middlebrook, one of the riflemen. He had a hole in his temple.

"My God," Sledge gasped.

A sergeant ran over. "Did he get shot by one of the Japs?"

Sledge couldn't answer.

The man who had crawled into the road to see who was groaning turned pale. With quivering lips, he went straight to the command post to report what had happened.

A little later that morning Captain Haldane appeared and, one by one, questioned the men who had been close enough to have seen at least part of what happened the night before. How many Japs? he wanted to know.

Two, Sledge told him. Only two.

Had Sledge seen who shot Middlebrook?

Yes, he had, Sledge replied.

Captain Haldane nodded. Sledge should keep that information to himself, he said. This had been a tragic mistake, and there was nothing now that would bring Middlebrook back. The Marine who shot him would feel it for the rest of his life.

Over the decades, those of us who know about the incident, who know who shot Middlebrook, have kept faith. Like those of us who know who killed the dog handler, it's never spoken of. When we get together, the last few of us, we don't talk about it.

━━━━━━

Headquarters had sent our regiment north along the west road because there was a change in strategy. Instead of tackling the Umurbrogols head-on, they had decided to move around behind them and come down from the north. Our job was now to secure the north end of Peleliu. Once this was done we'd start working our way down the ridges and valleys, digging the Japs out of their caves as we went.

The morning after the terrible night along the west road, we moved through the ruins of a small village that Second Battalion had taken the day before. Then we attacked and overran a steep hill that overlooked a trail connecting the island's west and east roads across a broad saddle. All the time we were taking Jap artillery fire from somewhere north of us and from a big gun over on Ngesebus Island. Every time it went off you could hear the *whump!* all over Peleliu.

North of our hill, a row of four round-topped hills extended across the island to the eastern shore. At right angles to these hills a ridge continued along the west road, overlooking the narrow channel that separated Peleliu from Ngesebus. Once the hills had been covered with thick trees, but we'd blasted them until they looked like they'd had a bad haircut. Still, they were full of hidden caves, and the caves were full of Japs. As long as they stood in front of us, there was no way to get at Ngesebus.

From the top of our hill we looked across a sixty-foot drop-off to the valley floor. On the hills opposite we could watch for Japs to appear in the cave openings and pick them off. And they could pick us off. There was a man on my left that afternoon, sitting about three or four feet away. I heard the *whack* of the bullet even before I heard the rifle shot. I knew instantly he was dead. I'd shot enough deer on the farm to know what a bullet sounds like when it hits. It got him about half an inch above his eyes, dead center.

There was no way to dig two-man foxholes, so once again we piled up rocks and hoped for the best. Normally we'd stay about six feet apart, almost at arm's length so we could reach out and touch one another. Through the night we'd take turns sleeping. I'd watch and the next man over would sleep. The man beyond him would watch and the next one would sleep, and so on.

When the Japs came calling at night they wore these rubber-soled canvas shoes, a little like sneakers. They didn't make a sound. You'd look out and not see a thing. You'd look the other way for a second and turn back. And there'd be a Jap right in front of you. Twenty feet away, where there was nothing at all before.

The fourth man down the line from me was sleeping. All of a sudden I heard this scuffle, these grunts, and then a long, drawn-out scream.

The guy had been sleeping flat on his back when he felt a weight on his chest and woke up with fingers around his throat. Afterward, when he was able to tell us what happened, he said he found this Jap sitting on him, choking him. He said he could feel himself going under, losing consciousness. He knew the man was going to kill him.

"Everything I was ever taught in training about judo, jujitsu, how to defend yourself ran through my mind like a streak of lightning," he told us. "I just went through everything.

"I knew what I was going to do. I reached up and put my left hand behind his head and with my right hand I poked two fingers in his eyes. Hard."

The Jap instantly released his hold and fell back.

"I grabbed him by the neck and the seat of the pants and threw him off the cliff."

I heard that Jap screaming all the way down, from the second his eyes were gouged until he hit the bottom. I've never heard such a bloodcurdling sound in my life.

The next day the Army moved into our places on top of the hill. We got word that evening that Third Battalion had been picked for a special operation. We were going across to Ngesebus.

CHAPTER 6

The Perfect Invasion

Ngesebus lay in plain sight. The channel separating it from the northern tip of Peleliu was about five hundred yards across and only four feet deep in places. There had been a wooden causeway between the two islands, but we'd bombed that out.

There was a small Japanese air base on Ngesebus, barely big enough for a Piper Cub, as well as the pair of big guns that had been pounding us across the strait. There was a chance that the Japs would barge reinforcements down from Babelthuap some night. At low tide they could easily wade across to Peleliu and surprise us like they had at Guadalcanal.

But for us, getting across was not going to be that easy.

The west road was the only approach. It ran to a phosphate refinery at the north end of Peleliu, passing along the foot of a low ridge. At right angles to the ridge a series of four round-top hills ran across Peleliu to the east coast. These hills were going to be a problem. But the real barrier to getting to Ngesebus was the ridge. Inside its northernmost tip the Japanese Navy had dug the granddaddy of all the cave-and-tunnel complexes. Entrances looked out in three directions with all sorts of cross tunnels and connections on several levels. It was equipped with electric lighting, communication lines, storerooms, and an infirmary. Everything the one thousand Japs inside would need to keep the west road bottled up and to survive an attack. Our planes and artillery hit that ridge over and over until we thought there was nothing left to hit. When the first of our tanks went clanking up the west road and into full view of the cave, the Japs fired down on it and stopped it dead. All this time the guns over on Ngesebus were also raining shells down on the north end of Peleliu. We had no way to launch an attack on the smaller island until we gained control of the ridge, the west road, and the channel beyond.

Someone at battalion headquarters hit on an idea—they blanketed the beach on Ngesebus with smoke shells, letting the clouds drift across the channel. Then five amtracs waded into the channel and turned their 75s on the hill. They targeted the largest cave entrance with round after round until return fire was silenced. Then, with tanks leading the way, an amtrac with a mounted flamethrower moved in and torched every cave opening they could find. As a final touch a team of engineers blasted the entrances shut.

Meanwhile we were waiting back at the junction of the west and east roads. Late in the afternoon we got word that the way was clear. We'd cross to Ngesebus at nine the next morning, September 28.

It could be that General Rupertus was embarrassed that the invasion of Peleliu had gone on long past the three days he had predicted. It could be that by now the division command was as frustrated with the place as we were and wanted to see some kind of clear-cut victory. But our assault on Ngesebus was planned to a tee. It was to be a textbook exercise. The next morning every senior officer on Peleliu and from the surrounding fleet who wasn't otherwise engaged was assembled at a point where they could look out over the channel and watch us go in. We had no idea we were playing to such distinguished spectators. They said afterward the reviewing stand must have been armor-plated.

We were at the north point of Peleliu, near the phosphate plant, by eight a.m. We boarded the amtracs and then, as usual, we waited. While we were waiting we were treated to a spectacular sound-and-light show by the Navy and our own fighter planes.

The battleship *Mississippi* and cruisers *Columbus* and *Denver* were parked out west of the strait, and for forty minutes they slammed the beach across from us from one end to the other with fourteen-inch and eight-inch shells. When that let up, the Corsairs started in. Two dozen had arrived from the *Lexington*, and boy, were we happy to see them. For the first time in the war, we had Marine pilots supporting Marine troops in a landing operation. They were taking off from the Peleliu airstrip and coming in from behind us. We watched as they peeled off, diving through the smoke and the dust, working the beach over with bombs, rockets and machine guns. As each plane finished its run it would fly back for another load. Some pilots cut it very close. We'd watch them dive and disappear into the columns of smoke. Just when we were sure they'd crashed, they'd pull into the clear, leaving the smoke swirling in their wake. Man, those guys were good!

The Corsairs were still at work at 9:05 when we started across, and they continued almost to the minute we drove up onto the sand and bailed out. Thirteen Sherman tanks led the way, waterproof for amphibious operation. Three were swamped, but the rest made it. We followed, packed into thirty-five amtracs. Most of them mounted 75mm howitzers and they were firing almost the whole way across. There were about seven hundred of us, all that was left of the Third Battalion. Two weeks ago, when we'd stormed ashore on Orange Beach Two, there had been a thousand. Like then, we were sweating and scared. Nothing on Peleliu had come easy. We were sure this wasn't going to be any different.

Ngesebus was even smaller than Peleliu, hardly a mile square, and flat except for one low hill. There were none of the high ridges and limestone cliffs that had made Peleliu a death trap. But Ngesebus had its own surprises waiting for us.

―――――――――――

It took the amtracs about six minutes to churn the five hundred yards. We expected any minute to run into the kind of firestorm the Japs had met us with on Peleliu's beaches, but there was only scattered fire from pillboxes and behind the few ragged trees the Navy and the Corsairs had left standing.

K Company was on the extreme left. This time we had the new model amtracs with the drop-down hatches in back. They rolled up on the beach and several yards inland before coming to a stop. We piled out and ran forward. Once again, the old lesson echoed in our heads: Get off the beach! Navy shells were landing farther inland now, and we had the airfield right in front of us, if you could even call it an airfield. The whole thing didn't amount to more than a single landing strip surfaced with crushed coral, and a crude taxiway. I'd be surprised if the Japs had ever landed anything bigger than a spotting plane.

We were still taking fire from among the scattered trees. A sniper winged one of our riflemen in the elbow, and when the mortar section corpsman, Ken Caswell, went to his aid, another Marine who was helpfully cutting the man's backpack free with his KA-BAR accidentally slashed Caswell across the face. The two men went back to first aid. We'd see both of them again.

In less than half an hour we made it across the landing strip and a few dozen yards beyond. There we came upon a low gray bunker that faced the channel.

Our orders were to set up our two guns on the far side of the bunker. K Company's gunny sergeant, W. R. Saunders, assured us it was clear. He said riflemen had already checked it out, dropping a couple grenades down a vent and moving on. So we went around it and started to dig in. About forty-five or fifty yards ahead, our other squad leader, Corporal Tom Matheney, and our sergeant, Johnny Marmet, were stringing phone wire to a forward observation post. I had no idea where Legs, our lieutenant, might be. That left me in charge, the only NCO on the scene.

After I had made corporal on Pavuvu I never fired the mortar again. I trained guys on it. But as squad leader my job was to be out front with the riflemen, observing and directing the gunner by phone, telling him how many yards to the target, how many degrees left or right.

I was working with good men. They had their quirks. But we were an effective team.

Private First Class George Sarrett, the guy I'd spooked with the land crab on New Britain, was one of the best Marines that ever put on a uniform. He was smart and fearless, and he was fiercely individualistic. I never had a bit of trouble from him, but I never saw him back down from anybody, either. I liked him because he was a fellow Texan.

Our gunner was Jim Burke. Gene Sledge, in *With the Old Breed*, called Jim a fatalist. I disagree. Jim was calm, like Sarrett. The only time I ever saw him get rattled was when Piss-call Charley bombed his foxhole on New Britain and he was calling over and over for a corpsman.

The assistant gunner was Private First Class Merriel Shelton. I'm the one who stuck Shelton with the nickname "Snafu." We were in the barracks at Camp Balcombe getting ready to go on liberty. Snafu was always talking, and when he'd get excited you couldn't always understand him. He was a Louisiana Cajun from down around Francisville, and he had that accent that kind of swallowed up his words.

That day he had his Australian money lying out on the cot. I said, "How much you got there, Shelton?"

He counted up the bills. "Well, I've got ten or eleven pounds," he said. Then he went through the small change. "And I must have eight or ten ounces."

I looked at him. "You're screwed up or something. You're just a snafu waiting to happen."

And that was it. From then on he was Snafu Shelton.

Whenever we got into a firefight Snafu would hunker down behind something and mutter over and over, "They need to send more men up here! We need more men here!"

I used to think, You get your ass up out of that hole and behind that gun and see what's going on, you might could take care of a few of them yourself. But I never said anything. Besides, he was a good man.

Private First Class Eugene Sledge was an ammo carrier. I never had to tell Sledge to do a thing twice. You asked him to do it, and he'd do it. He might be scared half to death, and a lot of the time he probably was. But he would do it. That's all you can ask of a man.

Private First Class John Redifer was our other ammo carrier. He was the type of person who likes to think things over. Slow and deliberate, but rock-solid. Nothing unnerved him. I never saw him panic. He and his buddy Private First Class Vincent Santos, a gunner and a Texan, used to go fishing on Pavuvu with hand grenades until somebody higher up put a stop to it.

All of these men were sure-enough Marines. I can't think of a higher compliment to pay them. You could count on them.

We'd been there around the bunker for a few minutes when Sledge called out.

"Burgin, there's Japs in this bunker!"

You never assumed your back was safe on Peleliu. We hadn't been watching our backs. Now, if Sledge was right, we had more than an isolated sniper behind us. We had a whole bunker full of them.

"I think you're cracking up, Sledgehammer," I yelled. "Saunders says it's clear."

Sledge, Vincent Santos, Snafu and Redifer were crouching in front of the bunker, watching several horizontal slits along its wall.

"I don't give a damn what Saunders told you," Sledge yelled back. "There's Japs in this thing. I can hear voices."

I went back to look over the situation. From what I could see, the low mound of coral sand about four feet high concealed a concrete box about twenty feet long and five feet wide. At each end steps led down behind an embankment and around a corner to a low entrance. You'd have to stoop to get in. The slits everyone had their eyes on were about eight inches long and two inches high with steel bars, like a jail cell.

"I could hear them jabbering in there," Sledge said.

I bent to look into one of the slits and a face looked back at me.

Before he could duck I stuck my M1 between the bars and got off two or three rounds. The face vanished. I'm sure I hit him. There was a sudden commotion in the bunker, like you'd hear from a beehive if you slapped a hollow tree.

I stuck the rifle in the slit again and emptied the clip, turning the barrel right and left, trying to get at every corner of that thing. Bullets were singing, ricocheting all over.

When the racket died down I could still hear jabbering. I couldn't tell how many there were in there. But I knew there had to be a bunch.

Just then a grenade came bouncing out of one of the side entrances. Everyone dove for cover as it went off. Two or three more grenades followed.

Redifer, Santos, Shelton and Private First Class Leslie Porter, another ammo carrier, climbed on top of the mound and the rest of us crawled around to the front—the beach side—and hunkered down.

"Sledge," I called out, "take a look in the end of that thing and tell me what you see."

Sledge poked his head over the embankment and ducked back. Instantly there was a burst of machine-gun fire from inside.

"You all right, Sledge?" I called out. He managed a weak croak, then disappeared around the corner of the bunker and climbed on top to join Redifer, Santos and Shelton.

Redifer was on his belly above one of the entrances when the barrel of a machine gun poked out. Before the gunner could fire, Redifer reached down and grabbed the barrel. The Jap jerked it back inside.

"There's an automatic weapon in here," Redifer shouted.

"It's just rifles," Snafu said.

That was Snafu. He could argue whether the sun came up.

While Snafu and Redifer bickered, Santos found a pipe sticking a couple inches above the bunker, probably the same one where Saunders's riflemen had dropped in their grenades. Santos started dropping grenades down the pipe as fast as he could pull the pins—and believe me, that was fast. Santos was a little guy but he was quick. When he ran out, Sledge and Snafu passed him their own grenades. We could hear a dull thump each time one exploded in the bunker below. It was hard to see how anybody inside could be alive after that. There was a moment of silence, then two Jap grenades flew out the side of the bunker. Most of us were clear, but Redifer and Porter, who were standing closest, raised their arms to shield their faces just as the grenades went off.

Both were peppered with fragments. Doc Caswell had returned, his face swathed in bandages. He worked over their forearms and soon had them patched up enough so they were able to go on. But I was thinking, This could go on forever. We're pinned down here. There's no need in getting my men killed. I motioned everybody back a few dozen yards to a couple bomb craters.

I knew one of the amtracs was idling down by the beach and it had a 75 mounted in a turret. I figured if we could get that amtrac to blast a hole in the bunker, we could make short work of the Japs and finish our business. While I was thinking, four or five Japs scrambled out of the bunker and took off to our right, running for a thicket. They were carrying rifles with bayonets, but they weren't shooting. What struck me as funny was they were running clutching their pants, which seemed half falling off. We cut them down before they got to the woods. I thought, What kind of army sends its men into battle without belts to hold up their pants?

I told everyone to stand by while I trotted down toward the beach. On my way I found Corporal Charlie Womack, I Company's red-bearded flamethrower specialist, and his assistant, Private First Class William Lewis. Lewis had a combat shotgun. Womack was broad-shouldered and big as a football lineman. He needed to be—he carried seventy pounds of napalm and nitrogen in tanks strapped to his back. I told him to wait while I got the amtrac. When I had rounded everyone up we rumbled through the brush the hundred yards or so back to the bunker.

"Here's what I need," I told the amtrac's gunner. "Knock me a hole in that thing at least two feet wide to where a flamethrower can get in and scorch 'em."

We ducked into the bomb craters to watch. The amtrac pulled closer to the bunker, then let loose with three or four deafening rounds that left our ears ringing for minutes afterward. Coral sand and chunks of concrete rattled down on us and the mortars. Seconds passed before we could make out anything through the smoke and dust. But sure enough, the 75 had done its work, opening a hole in the bunker about four feet wide. One shell had gone clean through. We could see through to the other side.

How anybody could survive that blast puzzles me to this day. But a Jap suddenly popped up in the hole, waving a grenade over his head and yelling something. Sledge and a couple others fired and he went down still clutching the grenade, which went off where he lay.

Now everybody was firing. "Get that flamethrower up here, Red," I yelled. "Everyone else, keep shooting!"

Flamethrowers are a wicked weapon, no doubt about it, but we never had any qualms about using them. They would do the job.

While we poured shots into the hole left by the amtrac, Womack and Lewis moved up to about five yards from the bunker. Lewis twisted a valve on one of the tanks. There was a jetlike *whoosh*, and a flash of heat and a torrent of orange flame splashed against the concrete and through the hole. We heard screams, and three more Japs came stumbling out the side, wreathed in flames. They went down in a burst of carbine fire, and as they lay writhing on the ground still burning, a couple of us ran forward to finish them off.

We waited for the smoke to clear, then Redifer and I ducked down and entered. Redifer was the kind of man you want with you in a situation like that.

When our eyes adjusted to the dark we could see why we'd had such a hard time digging them out of there. The whole length of the bunker was divided into a series of compartments separated by low openings. The openings were offset one from another so that a blast in one compartment would not reach the men in the adjoining compartments. Each had a narrow slit to the outside, a firing port. They could probably have holed up in there indefinitely, slipping out at night to bayonet us or slit our throats, like they had on Peleliu.

There were weapons scattered everywhere—a machine gun, rifles, grenades. We could smell charred flesh. In one of the compartments we found three or four blackened bodies heaped in a pile. The one sprawled over the top didn't look quite right. Something about the way he was lying there caught my attention—maybe I caught a slight movement. I motioned to Redifer to stop. Then I gave the Jap a kick in the ribs just beneath his arm. He grunted. I yanked my .45 out of its holster and fired into the back of his head, point-blank.

Altogether, we counted ten dead in the bunker, including the Jap

I'd just shot. Seven bodies lay outside. That was seventeen Japs that we knocked out without losing a man, two only slightly wounded. I felt pretty good about that.

For the rest of the day K Company mopped up the west end of the island, including a small hill north of the runway that was full of caves. We dug in late that afternoon at the foot of the hill, two to a foxhole, taking turns sleeping and watching. I shared a bomb crater with the guy who'd dropped the bazooka back on the first day on Peleliu. I took the first hour's watch, then he took over. The wind came up, carrying the sharp smell of smoke and burnt flesh. Sometime during the night a rain squall passed over. It was his turn to stand watch again and I gratefully fell asleep. For some reason I awoke in a short time. My companion was sprawled against the side of the crater, peacefully snoring. I sat on him and grabbed him by the lapels and slammed his head against the coral. Before he was half awake I had my hands around his throat.

"You son of a bitch," I said. "If ever I catch you asleep again when you're standing guard, you'll never wake up!"

After we got off Ngesebus, I went to Captain Haldane about the incident. I said, "I don't want that SOB in my platoon. Not if I can't depend on him."

We had one more day of fighting ahead of us, on a narrow peninsula jutting a few hundred yards to the northwest, where the Japs had located the big guns that had been giving us such fits. Three of our tanks knocked them out by early afternoon, and our invasion of Ngesebus was over. We'd faced about five hundred enemy defenders, but they were the best soldiers in the Imperial Japanese Army, veterans hardened by several years fighting in China and Manchuria. Our battalion lost forty-eight Marines—fifteen killed and thirty-three wounded. We'd killed 470 Japs. Only twenty-three had surrendered.

Late in the day the Army came across the island and relieved us. We boarded Higgins boats and went down the east coast of Peleliu to Purple Beach, where we would go into reserves. There we found Chesty Puller's First Marines, still waiting for a ship to take them to Pavuvu.

———————

As we were starting our rest, the Fifth Regiment's First and Second battalions were being thrown against the remaining Jap positions on the northern end of Peleliu. Second Battalion mopped up around the phosphate plant. First Battalion attacked and occupied the third of the four hills extending west to east across the island. The next day they turned their attention to the fourth and highest hill, which had a Jap radar on top. By late afternoon they were on the summit. The next day, September 30, they climbed into trucks and amtracs for the ride down the east road to the smaller claw, where they joined us at Purple Beach.

The last concentration of Japs on Peleliu were holed up in the rocky heart of the Umurbrogol, in a hellish jumble of coral rock called the Pocket. The only clear way into the Pocket was through a narrow valley called the Horseshoe that dead-ended in a steep slope, what Texans would call a box canyon. Beyond the Horseshoe was a seemingly endless series of ridges and valleys—Hill 140, Ridge 3, Boyd Ridge, Baldy, Wattie Ridge, Hill 120, Hill 100A. It went on and on.

In the center of the Horseshoe was a large sink that contained the only standing fresh water on the island. Japs would sneak out at night to fill their canteens here. The east wall of the Horseshoe was formed by a steep ridge that was anchored on the south by Hill 100. Hills seemed to be named for their elevation in feet. The ridge had been named for Lieutenant Colonel Walt, the regiment's executive officer who'd come looking for us the night we were lost in the scrub.

Overlooking the Horseshoe from the west was a row of crags and knobs starting with Five Sisters on the south, then Five Brothers. West of these was another valley, Wildcat Bowl. Beyond that rose a sheer cliff called the China Wall. The other side of that was Death Valley. From most of these ridges, the Japs could fire down on the west road.

For two weeks, the First Marines then Seventh Marines had thrown themselves at the Pocket, carving away slices from one side or the other until the Japs were pushed into an area no more than five hundred by a thousand yards. But this area was shot through with caves, most of them screened by thick brush. Our Shermans had advanced into the Horseshoe with the Seventh Marines and blasted every cave opening they could find. Then for some reason we never understood, headquarters had ordered the tanks withdrawn and sent back to Pavuvu. In their place came Shermans from the Army's 710th Tank Battalion. They

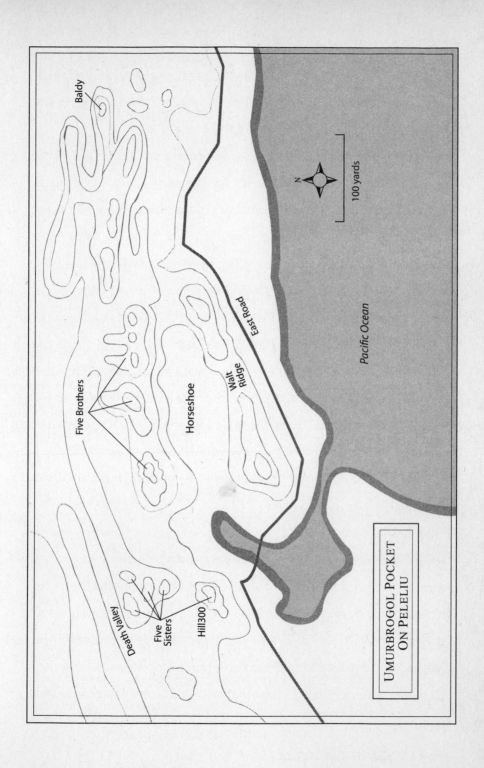

Baldy

100 yards

N

Pacific Ocean

East Road

Walt
Ridge

Five Brothers

Horseshoe

Death Valley

Five
Sisters

Hill300

UMURBROGOL POCKET
ON PELELIU

went in and pounded the same caves. Marine Corsairs dropped napalm, which burned off the covering trees until the ridges were as bare and scruffy as a mangy dog. That helped some.

On October 1 we got word to stand by to join the Seventh Marines for a final assault on the Pocket. The morning of October 3, trucks dumped us north of the airfield, where the east and west roads came together. We started west toward the Five Sisters. Our move on the Five Sisters was supposed to divert the Japs' attention from the Seventh Marines. Far to our right, they were moving down the east road to make another attack on Walt Ridge.

We led off with a heavy artillery barrage, then our Corsairs took over. They'd leave the airstrip, which was just behind us, and drop napalm on the rocky spires just in front of us. Then they'd wheel around, return to the airstrip and reload. The whole circuit couldn't have taken more than a minute or two. Most of the pilots didn't even bother to draw up their landing gear. It must have been the shortest bombing mission in the war.

Meanwhile we set up our guns and laid down heavy mortar fire in front of the advancing riflemen. They got to the first of the pinnacles about noon and within a few hours had taken four of the five. Their problem was the second pinnacle in the chain, which lay north of the others. To get to it, we had to squeeze between two of the other Sisters into Death Valley. We soon found out where it got its name.

Two weeks of fighting had stripped the trees bare and littered the ground with a knotted mess of tree limbs and rock. As we advanced, the Japs had a clear view from their caves up in the crags to our right. Our mortars were dug in a few dozen yards behind the riflemen, who were making good progress until, late in the afternoon, rifle and machine-gun fire started hitting them from everywhere at once. I'll say this about the Japs, they were disciplined. They'd hold their fire until we walked right into them.

The whole company was thrown back. There were calls for corpsmen everywhere. It got so bad that ammo carriers ran forward to help carry stretchers, leaving just a few of us to man the guns. Jap snipers seemed to single out corpsmen and stretcher carriers, and we tried to shield them by throwing smoke grenades. Every man's worst nightmare was that he would be hit while carrying a stretcher and dump a wounded Marine on the ground.

Before we got out of there, we'd lost five killed and fifteen wounded. It was K Company's worst day on Peleliu. We fell back and set up a new line just before sunset and waited for them to come creeping out of their caves. We were only a few hundred yards ahead of where we'd started out that morning. But we were in the open, where it would make it easier to spot infiltrators. During the night artillery fired star shells, which burst overhead, catching our visitors like a flashbulb. They came single or in pairs all through the night. At sunup we counted twenty-one dead Japs around us.

The next two days were the same story. We moved forward into the

Five Sisters, ran into intense fire and fell back. We lost nine more men, one of them killed.

All the time we kept up the mortar fire. George Sarrett and I were on the front lines, observing. Neither of us had caught a wink of sleep in three days. Just before it got dark I found I couldn't focus my eyes anymore. I called John Marmet on the phone.

"John, I gotta come in. I'm absolutely dead."

"Okay, come on in."

George and I scrambled back through the twilight until we got to where we'd set up the guns. There were two of them, each firing a round every two or three minutes, for harassment as much as anything. In front of one of the guns was a shell crater, and I flopped in. You get in front of a 60mm mortar, it's loud. The guns were firing right over my head every couple minutes all night long.

I don't even remember falling asleep. The next thing I knew Marmet was nudging me awake. It was eight o'clock the next morning. I'd slept in all that racket for twelve hours.

You get that way. You get to the point that you don't give a damn if you live or die, you're so exhausted. You're living in a nightmare. It's impossible to imagine the look and smell of a battlefield if you've never been on one, and impossible to forget if you have. The ground where we now found ourselves was littered with discarded combat gear, Jap rifles that we'd smashed so they couldn't be used again, spent shells, empty ammo boxes, bloody dressings, half-eaten rations rotting in the sun.

Half of us had diarrhea. You tried to dispose of it in empty ration cans and the like, but you were never far from the stink of shit. We and the Japs both tried to retrieve our dead, but too many times they were left where they fell. In the heat and humidity it didn't take them long to go sour, decaying and rotting and adding to the stench. Big metallic-green blowflies swarmed over everything. If you saw a corpse move, it would be maggots. Throw a rock into a bush and a cloud of flies would rise up thick enough to cast a shadow. They buzzed from the bodies and the shit. They were even crawling into our rations and into our canteen cups.

I don't know when it was that they finally started coming over in planes, spraying everything with DDT to keep down the flies. If it had any effect, we didn't notice. They were still thick as raisins.

Late one afternoon Sergeant Jim McEnery came upon the blackened and bloated bodies of four Marines in a ravine at the foot of one of the Five Sisters. They were laid out on stretchers as though somebody was carrying them to first aid. They'd been there at least two weeks.

A little later I found four more in a rock crevice. From their equipment I judged they'd been advance scouts from an intelligence unit. The Japs had hacked them to pieces. They'd cut off heads and hands. One of them, they'd cut off his penis and testicles and stuffed them in his mouth.

It made me dizzy and sick. We'd heard the stories. On New Britain

Japs had tied Marines to trees and used them for bayonet practice. So I never had felt any regrets about killing a Jap in combat. Never remorse about any of it. But after the sight of those mutilated bodies, I guessed I'd hate Japs as long as I lived.

While we were throwing ourselves against the Five Sisters, the Seventh Marines walked into a slaughter north of Walt Ridge that cut them up so badly they were pulled out. The regiment had lost 46 percent of its fighting strength and was in no condition to carry on. Trucks picked up the survivors and drove them back to the Purple Beach rest area. The First Marines had already pulled out for Pavuvu with over 70 percent losses. That left us. Peleliu had cost us 36 percent of our men, wounded and killed. But we were the only Marines General Rupertus had left.

Our commander, Colonel Harold "Bucky" Harris, had a well-known philosophy. Expend ammunition, not men. He had been rethinking the whole campaign against the Pocket. Whatever happened next, it wouldn't be another headlong rush. Under Colonel Harris, the Fifth would move slowly and deliberately, reducing the Pocket ridge by ridge and cave by cave. Foot by foot if necessary.

On October 6 Third Battalion was pulled back from the Five Sisters. At nine o'clock the next morning we went into the Horseshoe behind

Army tanks. Twice that day we pounded the lower slopes of Walt Ridge and the Five Brothers. Midmorning, when the tanks ran out of ammo, we withdrew to refuel and rearm. Then we went back in, this time taking demolition teams and amtracs with flamethrowers. We went on until early afternoon, when the tanks ran out of ammo again. Then we pulled out and were sent south for a rest.

About this time a three-day typhoon swept over Peleliu. The temperatures fell into the eighties, which was a blessing. But it turned the coral dust into gumbo. The mud clogged our equipment and everything bogged down. Supplies couldn't get in over the raging surf. Streams of Curtiss Commando cargo planes from Guam air-dropped essentials. After the storm passed temperatures shot up over a hundred again and the mud turned back into dust. Things were as they had been.

On October 10, K Company was pulled out of reserves and sent to clean out a nest of snipers who had been firing down on the west road. We were well behind the front lines, in territory that was supposed to be secure. But once again the Japs had hunkered down and waited. A week before, at a spot along the road called Dead Man's Curve, they had fired on an Army convoy and brought it to a stop. Everyone bailed out and ran for cover, ducking down behind trucks or diving behind rocks at the side of the road. Colonel Joseph Hankins, commander of First Division's Headquarters Company, had come along in his jeep to check on reports of snipers. When the convoy stopped, Colonel

Hankins got out and walked forward to see what was holding things up. Just as everyone yelled at him to get down, he was hit in the chest. He died lying there in the roadway, the highest-ranking Marine killed on Peleliu.

We had a couple Army tanks along with us this time to provide cover. We were taking rifle and mortar fire from several places along a cliff, but we couldn't see where it was coming from. Hillbilly Jones's rifle squad was just up the road, and as the morning dragged on a couple of his men were hit, and one of them was killed. Hillbilly decided to try to get a better view of the shooters from one of the tanks. I was about 150 feet away directing mortar fire and I didn't see everything that happened. But after discussing the situation briefly with a staff officer from battalion headquarters, Hillbilly climbed onto the back of the tank and scrambled forward to slap the side of the turret to alert the gunner what he was up to. He was just peeking around the turret when a single shot hit him in the side and knocked him down. He rolled off the tank into the road, and the call went out for a corpsman. While we watched, Hillbilly picked himself up, bleeding from the side, and pulled himself back onto the tank. Then he stood up. The next shot caught him in the chest and knocked him flat again. This time he didn't move.

Word spread down the line—Hillbilly's been hit. By the time I got to the tank, stretcher bearers had carried away the body. All the memories came flooding back. Hillbilly carrying his guitar down to our tents on Pavuvu. Lazy days singing and cracking jokes on the deck of a troopship. Guard duty drinking grapefruit juice and alcohol, and afterward the hangover, on Banika.

For the rest of the day and into the next we blasted away with machine guns, mortars, and rifle fire at every crack or opening we could find along the west road. We took plenty of fire in return, until eventually it tapered off. Not once during that time did we see a single live Jap.

The day after Hillbilly was killed, Second Battalion made it south all the way to the foot of Hill 140, at the head of the Horseshoe. By midafternoon they had taken it, and after that they held it against a sharp counterattack. The battalion had fought its way in from the east road past Baldy, where the Seventh Marines had been beaten so badly. This time bulldozers smoothed the way, clearing a path for flame-throwing amtracs and sealing caves as they advanced.

Command viewed Hill 140 as the key to the whole operation. Its west side fell away sharply to the floor of the Horseshoe. The top looked down on four of the Five Brothers, just to the south. K Company's mortars were rushed back along the west road and let out at a place where we could proceed on foot to Hill 140. There we would rejoin the rest of Third Battalion, which was on its way to relieve the Second Battalion early the next day. First Battalion had already gone into reserve. That left us the last Marine battalion fighting on Peleliu.

The death of Hillbilly Jones had been a blow. Soon we would absorb another.

Command's idea had been to plant a 75mm pack howitzer on the top of the hill. But the crest was too sharp and narrow for a gun emplacement, and soon both gun and crew had been dislodged by Japanese fire.

When the Third Battalion arrived, Second Battalion was taking fire from three sides. Where the hill dropped into the Horseshoe, there was no protecting flank. In effect, they held the hill on just three sides. The other was exposed. Orders for Third Battalion were to secure the south side and take the bend out of the line.

In the morning they started working their way up the hill to where Second Battalion was dug in just short of the crest. Everybody was warning them not to show their heads over the top. Jap snipers on the far side were alert, and deadly. But someone needed to see what was beyond the hill in order to direct the battalion's fire.

Captain Haldane, Johnny Marmet, Sergeant Jim McEnery and a couple other NCOs had made their way to the top and were flat on their bellies trying to figure out how to get a look at the other side. Second Battalion's own machine gunners were dug in so low, they could hardly see what they were shooting at. They had to sight their guns by looking under the barrels.

This was not satisfactory to Captain Haldane, who was himself an old machine gunner. He slithered forward a few feet and cautiously raised his head.

Everybody heard a sharp *thwack* and knew instantly what it meant.

Those who were close enough said his head just exploded. There was no point in even calling for a corpsman.

We had just arrived at the foot of the hill, looking for our new positions, when Sergeant Marmet came stumbling down the slope, a Thompson submachine gun dangling from his hand by the strap. I knew the moment I saw his face something had happened.

"Hey, Johnny," I said. "What's going on?"

He shuffled his feet and gazed off for a moment. "Okay, guys, let's get squared away here," he said. Then silence. We looked at one another.

"What the hell's wrong?" I asked.

"The Japs got the skipper a few minutes ago on the ridge," he said. It was like a kick in the stomach. Somebody threw down the base plate and the mortar tube. Somebody said, "Goddamn." Sledge turned away. We stood there paralyzed and silent.

Finally Marmet pulled himself together. "All right," he said. "All right. Let's move out." And we did.

It was more than a death in the family, losing Hillbilly Jones and Andy Haldane like that. They had been on Guadalcanal together, on New Britain and Peleliu. I found out later Haldane had been about to recommend me for the Silver Star for our action at the bunker on Ngesebus. He was killed before he could write it up. It didn't make things any better and it didn't make things any worse, as far as I was concerned. Hillbilly and Ack-Ack had been the core of our officers, leaders of men. Leaders of Marines.

First Lieutenant Thomas "Stumpy" Stanley was brought in from the battalion command post to take charge. The mortar squads were lobbing shells over the rim of Hill 140 into the northern end of the Horseshoe and at Walt Ridge beyond.

Jap artillery was answering us less and less. We got the feeling they were just waiting in their holes, like spiders. It rained off and on, and when the sun came out the rain turned to steam. The smell of death and the flies hung over everything, worse than ever. From where we looked out there wasn't a speck of green anywhere on the island. We'd stripped it bare. All that was left was gray rock and rolling smoke.

On the thirteenth, K Company advanced 150 yards and straightened out the lines. We spent part of the next day with demo squads, sealing caves and stringing communication wire to hinder infiltrators. We figured the more pressure we put on them, the more determined the Japs would be to infiltrate, or even to break out. We heard that the Eighty-first Army Division, the "Wildcat" Division, was on its way from Angaur to relieve us. We also heard that command had declared the assault phase of the invasion—whatever that meant—officially ended. It had been twenty-eight days since we came ashore on Orange Beach Two.

This is where we finished our war on Peleliu. At dawn on October 15, the Army troops marched in, looking grim. They had six more weeks of combat ahead of them. We were headed out. We boarded trucks to the north end of the island, where the Seabees had set up a new bivouac area. For the first time in months we slept in tents, and the tents had plywood decks, which we hadn't even had on Pavuvu. There were showers, a cookhouse, a mess tent where we could eat sitting down at tables. They had hung a sheet between trees where they could show movies. We shaved, washed our hair, brushed our teeth. Then we brushed our teeth again, just because we could do it.

This idyllic life didn't last long for the mortar section. We were sent out to the east road and told to set up our guns facing the sea, just in case the Japs tried a landing. (It was not such a far-fetched idea. We heard later the Japs sent a small force over from Babelthuap in mid-January. It was intercepted and all but two of the eighty or so invaders were killed.) A few miles to the south we could hear the Army's guns pounding away at the Pocket.

Finally they sent us down to Purple Beach to await transport back to Pavuvu. We were issued fresh uniforms, new boondockers, and that wonder of wonders, clean white socks. We burned the rags of our old uniforms and slept in hammocks, our sleep occasionally disturbed by tracers from the distant fighting. I dreamed of Florence, of the little bungalow we'd set up someday, of children running around the house.

A new cemetery appeared alongside the main runway at the airfield. Somewhere among the crosses Hillbilly Jones and Andrew Haldane were at rest. Altogether, the First Marine Division had lost more than 1,250 Marines on Peleliu. More than 5,400 had been wounded. There was no way to count the Japs, but we had killed more than ten thousand for certain. I read somewhere afterward that we had fired almost 16 million rounds of ammunition of all kinds during our time on Peleliu. That works out to more than 1,500 rounds per Jap. That seems about right.

The Fifth Marines had been the only regiment to achieve all its combat objectives. We had established our beachhead, crossed the airfield, occupied Ngesebus, secured northern Peleliu and whittled hundreds of yards off the Pocket. Of course none of us was thinking about any of this while we were at Purple Beach. We were just waiting for our ship to come in.

Transports arrived and one by one the other battalions departed, until we were the last Marine unit on the island. Finally, on October 26, the USS *Sea Runner*, a Navy troopship, appeared offshore.

The next morning Higgins boats took us out through heavy seas. The *Sea Runner* had thrown cargo nets over the side, and the little boats bucked on the waves while we tried to grab the nets and pull ourselves to. There wasn't much talk, no grab-ass going on. We hung on to the nets and started up, hand over foot. I had to stop and rest. We had full packs and the climb seemed to go up and up forever. At the top, sailors reached over and hauled some of us aboard who couldn't make it. We lay on the deck gasping. No doubt about it, we were a bunch of beat-up raggedy-ass Marines.

The day before we left Peleliu for the *Sea Runner*, K Company assembled on Purple Beach for a photographer. I have a framed print of the photo hanging in my living room right next to my KA-BAR, some plaques, a flag and some other Marine memorabilia. I look at it every so often. We're standing there in the strong morning light, on coral sand under swaying palm trees. There are about eighty-five of us, out of the 235 who landed on Peleliu. All of us are skinny. I weighed 138 pounds, down from 165 pounds when I joined the Marines. About half of us are shirtless. None are smiling. I'm the tall one standing right in the middle of the front row.

And you know what? I have absolutely no memory of having that picture taken.

CHAPTER 7

Second Battle of Pavuvu

We were a pretty quiet bunch for the six days it took us to sail from Peleliu to Pavuvu. A destroyer escort tailed us most of the way, a reminder that enemy submarines were lurking. Hillbilly Jones wasn't there with his guitar, so we didn't have our sing-alongs on the deck of the *Sea Runner*. There wasn't any point in polishing and repairing weapons. We were worn down and sobered. What we'd been through hadn't sunk in, and whatever it was we were heading to wasn't yet a reality.

Pavuvu looked about the same as we pulled into Macquitti Bay. We were returning to the same rows of tents, the same streets, the same palm trees, the same rats and land crabs, but they'd made a few changes.

The Higgins boats took us in to a new steel pier, so we knew the Seabees had been at work. The first thing we saw on the beach was half a dozen Red Cross girls, standing behind decorated tables. They offered us paper cups of grapefruit juice. I suppose it was somebody's idea of a welcome, but after what we'd been through it just hit me as the strangest thing on earth. What were they doing out here in the middle of the war? I walked on by, along with a few of the others. But Snafu and Santos headed straight for the girls.

They had started construction on a USO canteen near the beach. I never did visit it much, but it was there for those who wanted it.

We sat around until trucks drove us up to Third Battalion's bivouac area. They'd surfaced the grid of streets with crushed coral since we'd left, and the last of the rotting coconuts had been cleared away. The tents were new, with plywood decks. Seabags with our personal stuff had been piled in the center of each tent. As soon as we started unpacking, the land crabs came skittering out in every direction.

We had showers and a laundry and electric lights. The screened-in battalion mess hall had a concrete floor and rows of tables where we could play cards or just sit around in the evening. But most of us old-timers just went back to our tents, or wandered from tent to tent, looking for old buddies who were in different outfits. We found that many of them had not come back.

Some of the guys complained about the chow not being all that great. But if a Marine isn't complaining, he isn't happy. No, it wasn't Mom's home cooking. But it was good enough. And there was plenty of it. We weren't short. We had fresh meat, Coca-Cola and two cans of watery beer a week.

For those just off Peleliu who had spent so much time bitching about everything the first time around, Pavuvu looked pretty good by now. At least nobody was shooting at us.

We didn't do much of anything for the first ten days or so. They just let us alone to rest and regain our strength, and to mourn for those we'd lost. Then they started us to work, and that helped. Not to forget, but to put everything behind you, to move on. Gradually they picked up the pace and the training got harder. Our platoon now had three mortars and new guns were issued to replace those that had worn out.

While we had been at sea, the First Division was assigned a new commander. Major General Pedro del Valle replaced General Rupertus. General del Valle was a spit-and-polish man, and soon he was putting us through inspections and reviews and close-order drill on the resurfaced parade ground. Like I said, the Marines always knew which buttons to push.

We found our replacements from the States lounging around the tents. The First Division had about forty-five hundred new men to absorb, and we set to work immediately teaching them what we knew. We had now become the division's "old men." The Guadalcanal vets got ready for rotation back home. One night late in November Johnny Marmet came into my tent and sat on the cot.

"You know your promotion to sergeant is in the works," he said.

"Yeah, I knew that," I said. "Thanks for recommending me."

That's when he told me that Captain Haldane had been about to write me up for a Silver Star.

We said our good-byes, and he left. I would miss Johnny. He was one of the best.

Since it looked like I would be replacing him, I set about reorganizing the mortars. I needed a couple ammo carriers. I'd met some of the new replacements and found out that two of them were from Texas—T. L. Hudson and Clyde Cummings. I went down to the end of the company street to the sergeant in charge and told him I wanted both men for my platoon.

"Oh, you do, do you?" he said. "Just why in the hell do you want those particular two?"

"Well, in the first place they're Texans," I said. "In the second place, both are good, strong young men. I need two good ammunition carriers and they can do the job. And I want them in my platoon."

He laughed. "Yeah, go on and take them."

They were good men, and I put them to good use.

Florence's letters caught up with me, and I was writing her whenever I got time, two or three times a week. I couldn't say much. Our mail was censored. We couldn't write anything about where we were or where we'd been or what we were doing. Just, Hello, I miss you terribly, I love you, I hope to see you soon, Good-bye.

I wrote Florence that if I had my pick of babies, I would like a little girl. She said she told her mother that she planned to have a dozen boys. I kept having dreams that we were married already, living in a little house back in Texas. I longed to wake up and find her in my arms. My letters were short, two or three pages. I could never think of anything to say. Hers were long, six pages and more, and full of news from Australia. She sent me newspapers. One day a fruitcake arrived. I took a piece down to Jim Burke, and when I got back to my tent the rest of the guys had cleaned out every crumb. I told them the next time Florence sent a cake they wouldn't even know about it.

Our battalion had organized a volleyball team and a basketball team, and I wanted to play on both, but they usually had games at the same time. So volleyball won out. We also played baseball and we had boxing matches. The evening before Thanksgiving they showed a movie. Afterward I just sat there for half an hour listening to records, and then I went back to my tent. Some nights on Pavuvu were just beautiful, with a huge moon hanging over the sea. I would have enjoyed them if only I had Florence there to share them.

President Roosevelt had proclaimed November 23, 1944, a day of national thanksgiving. I gave thanks I was still alive to think about my loved ones even if I couldn't be with them. "I am a very happy yet a lonesome boy," I wrote to Florence. We had six boxing matches during the day, then turkey with all the trimmings. Afterward there was an amateur talent show, another movie, and cold drinks.

We didn't know it yet, but the week before Thanksgiving the Army's Eighty-first Division Wildcats had wrapped things up on Peleliu. Colonel Kunio Nakagawa, the Japanese commander, radioed his headquarters on Babelthuap that it was "all over." All he had left in the Pocket was 120 men and most of them were wounded. He and his aide burned the ceremonial colors and, as we knew they'd do all along, committed ritual suicide.

So we could take pride in a job well done.

———

I guess I had something else to be thankful for. Legs, the lieutenant who had given me so much trouble for so long, had been transferred. Our new mortar section leader was Lieutenant Robert Mackenzie, a blond New England college kid fresh out of Officer Candidates School. We called him Scotty.

In *With the Old Breed*, Gene Sledge was pretty hard on Scotty, but I didn't share his hard feelings. Scotty and I were good friends then and we stayed good friends right up until he died in 2003.

Sledge was right about one thing, though. Scotty certainly came to Pavuvu with a gung ho attitude. Right away he made it plain that he was one tough Marine. The first time the Japs hit, he assured us, he'd charge them with a KA-BAR clenched in his teeth and a .45 clutched in his hand. He was going to do this and he was going to do that. It was comical to us—some of us had already faced the Japs. We knew better.

I think in the beginning Scotty actually believed it himself. We tried to set him straight, but he wasn't listening. Guys like him grew up in a hurry. He'd come right out of OCS into the combat area. He hadn't been around veterans. The only thing in his mind was what he had seen in the movies. It was just the rookie in him talking. I thought he was green as a gourd.

Still, I liked him. Later on I'd get so mad at him sometimes I'd want to kill him. Then thirty minutes later he'd have me laughing about something so hard I'd forgotten all about it. But he did pull some dumb things.

Late in December after my sergeant's commission came through, they started calling some of us up to interview us for field commissions. Those chosen would be made second lieutenants. I'd been interviewed for Officer Candidates School on New Britain, but I had not attended college and that was the end of that. Now my chance for promotion came again.

After lunch I put on fresh khakis and went down to headquarters, where they were holding interviews. There were four of us, myself, Hank Boyes and Ted Hendricks from K Company, and a guy I didn't know from L Company.

A first lieutenant met me and ushered me inside. There was a long table with three or four officers from captain on up sitting along either side. I wasn't nervous. If they wanted to make me an officer, that was fine. But I wasn't seeking it. They made me feel at ease and asked me to sit at the head of the table.

There were a lot of questions. How did I like the Marines? I said I liked the Marines just fine. They asked about my combat experience, and what did I feel about ordering men into action, where they might be killed? I said I was okay with that. I had done it before when I'd sent men out to be stretcher bearers.

One of them asked if I planned to make the Marine Corps my career.

I said, "No, sir, I'm not making the Marine Corps a career."

"Why not?"

"Well, sir, I joined the Marine Corps to fight the Japs. And whenever we whup their butts, I'm going home."

Another officer was looking over some papers. "Have you been saving any money since you joined the Marine Corps?" he asked.

"Yes, sir, I have."

"And you've been sending money home?"

"Yes, sir, I have."

He repeated the question. "And you're sending money home?"

"Yes, sir, I am."

"How much money have you sent home?"

I knew the exact figure. "Over two thousand dollars, sir."

"Two thousand dollars?"

"Yes, sir."

"Hmmm." He tapped his finger on the table. "You've been a private, a private first class, a corporal and a sergeant. You were making fifty-five dollars and you're now drawing sixty-five dollars a month. And you've sent two thousand dollars home?"

"Yes, sir."

He said, "Sergeant Burgin, do you shoot crap?"

"No, sir, I do not."

"You have that kind of money going home. You sure you don't shoot crap?"

I said, "No, sir."

He didn't ask if I played poker.

The truth of it was, I was sending ten dollars a month home, plus whatever money I won in poker. I was far from a skillful poker player compared to some of them in the company. We had about five or six guys that were the *real* poker players. And they didn't even start until about a week or ten days after we got our paychecks. They'd hold back and let these little games like I was in run their course, letting the money gather. *Then* they'd play poker. Big fish eating the little fish.

Maurice Darsey, our first sergeant, and Snafu were our regulars, the real players. For a time I was company clerk. Mo would give me $1,000 and tell me to go to the post office and buy money orders. I had to buy ten because you couldn't get a money order for more than $100 at the time. So I'd buy ten money orders and bring them back and Mo would put them in an envelope and mail it home. He'd say, "Ah, that's another mule on the farm."

We played poker mostly evenings in the tents. And it was a rare tent that didn't have a coffee can of jungle juice brewing somewhere out in back. We'd take any kind of dried fruit we could get our hands on, usually raisins, prunes or apricots. Put a little sugar and water in, partly seal it and let it ferment. Some of the guys would hang their can in a palm tree. In a week or so it would be ready.

Jungle juice was pretty bad stuff, but it would do the job. I remember the first time T. L. Hudson, a private and ammo carrier, got drunk on that stuff, maybe the first time he got drunk in his life. Some Marines had a can of jungle juice they'd made with dried peaches. They'd already drunk all the juice, and there was nothing left in the can except the fruit at the bottom. Hudson kept sticking his hand in there, pulling out those alcohol-soaked peaches and eating them. We called him "Peaches" for a long time after that.

Four times a year, the Marine Corps would lay out a feast for the men—Thanksgiving, Christmas, New Year's Eve, and November 10, the anniversary of the creation of the Corps. We had refrigeration units on Pavuvu now, so we had fresh meat a couple times a week, plus a kind of mutton stew we called "corn-willie."

For Christmas they brought over turkeys from Banika and roasted them, with dressing, mashed potatoes, gravy, pea soup, cranberry sauce, apple pie and coffee. While we ate, the loudspeakers played Bing

Crosby Christmas carols and big-band music by Glenn Miller and Tommy Dorsey.

Tommy Dorsey brought up old memories. Back at Camp Elliott near San Diego, whenever we got weekend liberty a buddy and I would hitchhike up to Los Angeles. In those days anybody would pick you up if you were in uniform. On Saturday nights we would go to the Hollywood Palladium. They had all the big-name bands there. I remember Tommy Dorsey played two nights, and one of the nights Betty Grable was in the club. I was just another lowly Marine, rubbing shoulders with all that Hollywood glamour.

For New Year's Eve, the Corps repeated the turkey feast. Someone decided we were going to get at least one of those turkeys, maybe two, and bring them back to K Company. I don't remember everyone who was in on that scheme, but I know Peter Fouts and Howard Nease were involved, both corporals. Fouts had been wounded in the arm by a machine gun on the beach at Peleliu, but he had recovered and was back with us. Nease would soon be killed by shrapnel on Okinawa.

We finished dinner and were back in our tents when we heard cries of "Fire! Fire!" We looked out and saw a bunch of people running around the battalion mess hall. A pretty good fire was going in a brush pile near the entrance.

Later that night somebody shook my shoulder, waking me up. "Psst, Burgin! You want some turkey?"

I said, "Yeah, yeah."

"Well, come on!" I hopped off my cot and followed him to a nearby tent, where everybody was sitting around eating turkey and drinking beer. Nease carved off a couple slices with his KA-BAR and handed them to me while they told and retold the whole story.

It seems somebody had carelessly left a can of gasoline in that brush pile. While the mess crew was cleaning up after supper, the brush had mysteriously burst into flame. The sentry on duty yelled "Fire!" and while everybody was running around trying to put it out, two leftover turkeys vanished from the galley.

We finished our midnight snack.

"Make damn sure you don't leave any of this stuff lying around," somebody reminded us. We took the bones and carcasses over to I Company's bivouac and dumped them in their trash can.

Guess who got the blame the next day for stealing the turkeys.

––––––––––––––––

As the new year began the rumor mill kicked into high gear. There were the usual stories that somebody had shot himself. For a time there was speculation that the Marines were about to be absorbed into the Army. That one had popped up again and again over the years. There was a tale they were putting saltpeter into our food to cool down our sex drive. I don't know what they thought we might do, with only a handful of Red Cross girls on the island, safe behind barbed wire most of the time. Our tents were about three-quarters of a mile from the beach, and I didn't bother to go down to the USO canteen just to be hanging out there. From time to time I'd go to company headquarters to visit a friend of mine I'd gone to school with. Whenever I went down there I'd see the Navajo code talkers hanging around, but I never got acquainted with any of them.

Mostly the rumors were about where we were going next.

Our training now emphasized street fighting and mutual support between tanks and infantry. That led some of us to think that we were headed for Formosa or mainland China, or even to Japan itself. There was a map of a long, narrow island in circulation, but none of us recognized it.

In late January the whole division shipped out to Guadalcanal for amphibious maneuvers in LCIs—Landing Craft, Infantry. These were a newer and smaller version of the LSTs we'd taken to Peleliu, but with ramps running down the side instead of bow doors. They could carry an infantry company plus a couple of jeeps. We'd go out and make a run for the beach. When we got on shore we'd bail out and move in a few dozen yards. Then we'd get back on the LCIs, go out and do it all over again, eight or ten times a day. The mortar platoon also practiced setting up with three guns until we could do it in our sleep.

Guadalcanal had the same long, thick kunai grass we'd seen around the airfield at Cape Gloucester. It reminded me of the Johnson grass back home. In the grass we found these big lizards, about two feet long, with flickering tongues, like a snake's. The natives called them goannas, and we had a lot of fun with those things. When we came up on one we'd all gather around a circle daring each other to grab him. Of course when that rascal came charging, we all gave him plenty of space.

All this time we were listening to the Armed Forces Radio Service, so we got word whenever the Marines hit another island. I didn't know how many of those islands there were out there, but I knew every one of them was on the way to Tokyo. We'd gone from Guadalcanal in 1942 to Tarawa, to Kwajalein, Saipan, Guam and Peleliu. When we returned to Pavuvu from maneuvers, the Third, Fourth, and Fifth divisions invaded Iwo Jima. We listened closely to every news report. Once again the Japs had holed up in caves and fought to the last man. It sounded a lot like what we had been through on Peleliu, but shorter and with three times the casualties. We knew we would be next. And we knew we were in for a helluva fight.

In February we went back to Guadalcanal for two more weeks of exercises and maneuvers off Tassafaronga Point, where the Navy had suffered a big defeat by the Japs in 1942. They worked us even harder, adding cliff climbing to our exercises because, they said, we would be climbing a seawall to get onshore at our next destination. We camped in what had been the Third Division's bivouac before they left for Iwo Jima and hoped that wasn't an omen.

During our stay on Guadalcanal some of us discovered the Seabees' mess hall, where the chow was better and more abundant than what the Marines had been feeding us. The Seabees were pretty generous, allowing us to join the chow line after they had been through.

T. L. Hudson—"Peaches"—and I discovered the PX at Henderson Field, where we could buy ice cream bars, something we'd never seen on Pavuvu. They were four inches long, two inches wide and half an inch thick, covered with chocolate, and they cost a nickel. We thought we'd died and gone to heaven. T.L. and I would get in line and buy one each—they'd only sell you one at a time. We'd eat those then get in line and get another one. Then we'd come back around again. They never caught on or they didn't mind. Either way, we made four or five trips through that line.

We almost didn't make it off of Guadalcanal. At the end of the last day of maneuvers, our squad waited on the beach for the Higgins boat that was to take us back out to our mother ship, the USS *McCracken*. We were dog tired. The sun was getting lower and lower until we were the last bunch left on the beach. The wind had come up and the sea was getting choppy. Finally the boat came nosing in and dropped its ramp on the sand. We climbed aboard wearily and stowed our weapons. The bay was full of ships, and we passed several on our way out, bouncing on the waves. I looked down and saw water sloshing beneath the deck. We were overloaded and taking on water. I went forward and told the coxswain, "We better get this thing to a ship." He took one look and turned toward the nearest ship. Meanwhile the water was coming up under our feet and the Higgins boat was riding lower and lower in the waves. The coxswain started the bilge pumps. We pulled alongside an attack transport and yelled for help. They yelled back, asking where we were from and what was the problem. Our coxswain explained that we were from the *McCracken* and we were taking on water and they threw a couple lines down to us. The water was creeping up our ankles now. As our boat started going down we got the lines attached. We scrambled up the cargo net and spent the night on the transport. The next morning a Higgins boat took us back to the *McCracken*.

————————

Things were moving faster. The *McCracken* took us not to Pavuvu, but to Banika, where we spent a week loading ships and getting the usual round of inoculations that come before a major campaign. Troopships began appearing offshore. On March 14 we boarded the *McCracken* again and the next morning sailed out of the harbor and north to Ulithi.

Ulithi had been secured without a fight by the Army's Eighty-first Wildcat Division about a week after we went ashore at Peleliu. It was really a cluster of small islands surrounding a deepwater port, where the fleet for our next operation was coming together.

We knew by now we were headed for Okinawa. For once they didn't wait until we got on board ship to tell us. Scotty showed us a map of the island. It was only 350 miles from Tokyo.

Now we understood why they had pushed street fighting and tank warfare in our training. Unlike Cape Gloucester and Peleliu, Okinawa had a lot of open cultivated ground, including not just villages but real towns.

If we hadn't been told, we would have known anyway that this was going to be bigger than any operation we'd had so far. From the deck of the *McCracken* all we could see was ship after ship, hundreds of them spread all the way out to the far horizon. It was as though they had assembled the entire U.S. Navy at Ulithi, from the biggest battleships and aircraft carriers down to escorts and patrol boats.

While we were at Ulithi, the battered hulk of the USS *Franklin* limped in and docked right next to us. I was standing only thirty or forty feet away. While we had been under way to Ulithi on March 19, a single Jap bomber had appeared out of the clouds and dropped two five-hundred-pound bombs on the carrier. She was just fifty miles off Kyushu, the westernmost of Japan's main islands. The bombs went right through the flight deck and exploded in the hangars, setting off ammunition and fuel. Almost 725 of her crew died and more than 250 were injured. We heard that many of the wounded were still on board.

The survivors fought the raging fires, dodging exploding bombs and ammo, and managed to bring the ship hundreds of miles into Ulithi. She was listing 13 degrees to starboard when they got her docked, so we had a close-up view from the deck of the *McCracken*. Her sailors were crowded on her ruined flight deck, leaning against the tilt. Smoke still oozed from her side where the explosions had torn holes the size of a garage door. It wasn't hard to imagine what the *Franklin* and her crew had been through. I guess every sailor who ever lived is also a firefighter. I had watched them hold drills on our transports. Every man knew exactly what to do and when to do it. I thought, At least on land we could dig foxholes and had some room to maneuver. On shipboard, there's nowhere to go.

While we were in port at Ulithi a telegram came for me, from Jewett, Texas.

My younger brother, Joseph Delton Burgin, had joined the Army the year before and after basic training had been sent to France. Before he enlisted, J.D. had written to me asking about the Marine Corps. I had written back to discourage him. I thought he might have an easier time of it than I did if he joined the Navy. But I guess we were all in harm's way, whether we were in the Marines or the Army or Navy.

Typical of J.D., he made up his own mind.

He was almost four years younger than me, always quiet, not a hell-raiser. But he would not be pushed around. When someone got in his face, you'd see those black eyes snapping in anger. When he was starting first grade, Momma made him a pair of overalls out of uncolored denim from cotton sacks. She had dyed them blue, so they looked like regular overalls. One morning she saw him sitting out on the porch cutting something with a pair of scissors.

"What are you doing out there, J.D.?"

"These overalls are hot, Momma. I'm cutting holes in them."

She chased him all the way across the yard and under the fence, where he got hung up on the barbed wire.

J.D. and I used to go fishing together, and possum hunting at night with the dogs and a .410 shotgun. He was with me when I shot my first deer.

According to the telegram, J.D. had been killed by German artillery in Alsace-Lorraine. An Army officer wrote my folks that it had been sudden. J.D. hadn't felt a thing.

—————

Nights on the deck of the *McCracken* were cool and pleasant as we sailed north from Ulithi. We could almost forget we were getting closer to Japan. But a briefing from K Company's officers sobered us right up. Okinawa would be the bloodiest campaign of the war, they warned us. We could expect 80 to 85 percent casualties.

Going in we would face heavy fire from a large Jap gun on the beach. Enemy paratroopers might drop in behind us, and there would probably be a banzai attack during our first night ashore. We were also facing a new tactic. Starting in October of 1944, Japanese pilots had been deliberately crashing their planes into American warships in a kind of aerial banzai attack.

The convoy that left Ulithi March 27 was the largest ever assembled in the Pacific. We had almost 1,300 ships of all kinds and more than

180,000 men from five Army divisions—the Seventy-seventh, Ninety-sixth, Twenty-seventh, Seventh and Eighty-first—and the First, Second and Sixth Marine divisions. We were facing at least 100,000 Jap troops who, we knew, would fight to the last man. Their back was to the wall.

The old bivouac rumor about the Marines being absorbed into the U.S. Army almost came true, in a way. The entire invasion force, called the Tenth Army, was under the command of Army Lieutenant General Simon Bolivar Buckner.

Because the Fifth Marines' Third Battalion had been in the first wave at Peleliu, we were to be spared that distinction at Okinawa. We'd be held offshore in regimental reserve.

It had now been sixteen months and a couple days since Florence and I sat on that park bench in Melbourne kissing and saying our good-byes. I was no closer to returning for her as I'd promised, no closer to settling down in our little house together. In fact each island where I'd fought took me farther from her. How long would I be on Okinawa? And then where? Japan? We knew as we were getting closer that the enemy was getting weaker and more desperate. Standing there at nights on the deck of the *McCracken*, I just couldn't see any end to it.

CHAPTER 8

April Fools

We awoke once again to the smell of steak and eggs from the galley. Sunrise was still two and a half hours away, but crews aboard the *Mc-Cracken* were already at their battle stations. Jap planes did not wait for the light of dawn before starting their bomb runs and kamikaze attacks. We'd been warned the night before to get plenty of rest because April 1 was going to be a long, hard day. I had slept pretty good, but I'd been through this twice before, three times if you count Ngesebus. Losing sleep did not make any landing easier.

It was Easter Sunday. And it was April Fools' Day. After the usual clatter and commotion of getting everybody up and collecting our gear, we assembled for a chapel service. I don't remember any of the details or what was said to us. But I'm sure many of us prayed very sincerely that morning. We stood in line for the mess hall, stood in line for the heads, and by twos and threes climbed to the deck.

The temperature was in the mid-seventies. It was going to be the kind of balmy, clear morning that back home would have sent me out into the woods with the dog and my hunting rifle. J.D. would probably have come along. The ship faced east and as the horizon got brighter, we could make out a long, low landmass silhouetted a few miles away with an umbrella of smoke hanging over it. We could hear the hum of airplanes getting closer and the bark of ack-ack guns from other ships. For several days we had watched as streams of plump B-24s droned high above, paying an advance call on Okinawa, but this time the approaching planes weren't ours.

"All troops below!" some sailor yelled. "No troops on deck! Captain's orders. Jap planes coming! We don't want Marines killed on our deck. Everybody get below."

Did the Navy think we'd never been under fire before? Swabbies were always hassling Marines. You'd find a shady cubbyhole to snooze and the first thing you knew some swabbie would come along with a hose to wash down the deck. We figured this was more of the same.

The *McCracken*'s 40mm antiaircraft guns started bellowing. Over our heads the silhouettes of planes came snarling over, swooping and darting like barn swallows. Flashes popped among them, and inky blots of smoke drifted away.

We were herded through a hatch and a sailor slammed it shut. The space we found ourselves in was dark and crowded. We were wearing full packs, and there was no ventilation. Before long we were hot as blazes. We could hear the racket above our heads and none of us wanted to be caught like pigs in a pen if a Jap plane or bomb came crashing through the deck. We started yelling for someone to let us out. Finally a bunch of us took matters into our own hands and battered the hatch open and we all came swarming out, the battle going full blast around us.

A Naval officer appeared on the deck above and behind us. "All Marines, return to quarters!" he barked. "That's an order! Do it now!"

"Sir, we're about to hit that beach. We'd just as soon take our chances out here."

He turned and strode away. While we milled around waiting for what might happen next, a couple of our own officers showed up and ordered us to stand by for loading. We formed up at the railing four abreast and waited for the signal to turn and scramble down the cargo nets. Climbing those things you try to make haste carefully. You hope the guy above you doesn't step on your hands or face, and you try to not step on the hands or the face of the guy below you.

When the amtrac was full, I called out, "Shove off, Coxswain. You're loaded." We nosed away from the ship and joined the line of other amtracs headed out to the assembly point just outside the reef until the signal came to form up and go in.

While we waited we watched the air show. A Jap plane nosed over and fell toward the sea, twisting and trailing a long spiral plume of smoke until it smacked the water. Another burst into flame and disappeared behind the hulk of the *McCracken*. Hellcats went weaving through the smoke and din, and we held our breath hoping the gunners on those ships knew their planes and aimed accurately. A lot of shipboard gunners, we knew, were our guys, Marines.

The Navy's big guns and rocket-launching LSMs were still working over the beach and beyond, planting long, even rows of explosions along the shore. Thunder swept across the waves and beat against our faces. Amtracs and Higgins boats headed this way and that. Many had already left troops on the beach and were headed out for another load or for supplies. The Fifth Marines' First and Second battalions were already landing on Blue Beach to our left. Our battalion was to have been held back in regimental reserve. But obviously they were sending us in along with everyone else to anchor the left flank on Yellow Beach. To the south a muddy river, the Bishi Gawa, separated us from Purple Beach, where the Army's regiments were coming in.

When the flag dropped we formed a wide line and started across the reef. Ships were pumping out clouds of white smoke, screening our approach. A few gray spikes erupted in the water in the distance. But so far we hadn't seen any of the burning amtracs that had made the trip into Peleliu such a nightmare. The Navy bombardment had ceased. In the quiet we could hear the rumble of amtrac engines all around us. Little by little Okinawa appeared through the haze and smoke. From my perch on the gunwale, I could make out ground sloping up from the beach and a patchwork of fields separated by rows of pine trees. Except for columns of rising smoke here and there it looked like nice farm country, a little like the countryside around Melbourne.

"Hey, we're not taking any fire!" somebody noticed.

"Yeah. You're right. Where are the Japs?"

Somebody yelled from the boat on our right, "We're going in unopposed." We passed the word to the boat on our left, and the news traveled all along the line, boat to boat. "Unopposed landing!"

"I don't believe this!" somebody else yelled.

No bodies floated in the water. No snipers' bullets whined over our heads. Just the steady beat of the amtrac's diesel and the churn of water against the hull.

They hadn't held our company in reserve because the whole landing was running so smoothly. They didn't figure they'd need us later on.

In our relief, somebody started singing "Little Brown Jug." We all joined in.

Ha, ha, ha, you and me,

Little brown jug, don't I love thee!

It had been one of Hillbilly's favorites.

Still, I was thinking, This can't go on. Something's got to go wrong here.

Nothing did. We motored on in. As we got close to the shore, we looked for the seawall that we'd spent all that time preparing to climb. There was a broken line of stones with gaps, like somebody's bad teeth, but no wall. If there had been one to begin with, the Navy's guns had punched it out. Farther in we could see the blackened hulk of a big artillery piece that had once pointed seaward. Our amtrac crawled out of the surf and through a gap between the stones. Then it stopped. The back gate slammed down and we piled out, ducking low out of habit. No shots came our way. It was more like one of our maneuvers than any battle we'd been through. We formed a line and began advancing across the beach. We heard occasional fire far to the left or right. But we were on our feet, moving calmly. There were plenty of shell holes to dive into if we had needed them. But we didn't. We'd walked ashore like we were strolling down the driveway to pick up the mail.

There was some action elsewhere along the lines. In the afternoon a sniper shot Colonel John Gustafson in the arm just as he stepped off an amtrac. He turned around and calmly walked back aboard and was taken out to the ship for treatment.

Marines still argue: Which was worse, Peleliu or Okinawa? I vote Peleliu, but others who went through both will tell you that Okinawa was worse, an opinion they base on the amount of artillery the Japs threw at us. After the first two or three days on Peleliu, we didn't get much of that—we'd knocked out most of their heavy guns. But on Okinawa, once it started, it just kept coming at us right up to the last days.

The Japs had learned from Peleliu. When we finally cornered them on Okinawa, once again they were holed up in caves and tunnels. We had to pry them out one by one, as we had on Peleliu. Lieutenant General Buckner called it a "blowtorch and corkscrew campaign." They were fighting on home ground. Okinawa is in the center of the seven-hundred-mile chain of islands stretching from Formosa to Kyushu, the Ryukyus. The Japs considered the whole chain part of their home islands, just like we might think of the Florida Keys. On Okinawa we faced everything we had faced on other islands all over again. Rain, mud, malaria, flies, bodies crawling with maggots. And we were tired. Before it was over, the fight for Okinawa would seem to stretch out to forever, with no end in sight.

But the first days gave us no hint of what was to come.

The area behind the beach was jammed with amtracs and DUKWs bringing in supplies, and we moved off quickly. The island was about six miles wide where we came in, and the plan was for us to cut it in half. The First and Sixth Marine divisions were to capture Yontan, the larger of two airfields. Then the Sixth Marines would turn north and sweep up the island to the tip. We would head directly across to the eastern shore. The Army meanwhile would capture the smaller Kadena airfield and turn south. All this was supposed to take a couple weeks. But by the time we were off the beach, troops had already moved up to the edge of both airfields.

The mouth of the Bishi Gawa River, where our mortar platoon landed, was choked with the wreckage of small boats. Some of them were the plywood suicide motorboats that had been caught by our planes before they could get out to our fleet. We advanced in a column past fields that had recently been harvested and were ready for the plow. The Okinawans grow rice and beans, yams and patches of sugarcane. It appeared they just let their livestock run free, because we kept encountering goats, pigs and chickens. We had some fine barbecues in prospect. The small farmhouses had thatched roofs, and looked tidy and well kept behind low stone walls. Yards were shaded by pine trees. But the buildings themselves were deserted. We found out later the Japs had been telling the natives tales of what terrible things the Americans, especially the Marines, would do to them.

As we walked by, I checked out their horses. They were smaller and shaggier than the ones I was used to back home, more like a Shetland than a true horse. They turned out to be gentle little horses, good work animals. And while I don't remember anybody trying to ride one, our mortar squad adopted one and soon had him carrying our ammo.

By afternoon we got to higher ground and began to catch occasional fire. Usually it was just a couple Japs on a Nambu light machine gun or a mortar, or a sniper. We'd knock them off as we came on them, and then run into another one a little farther along. But it seemed half-hearted, nothing like we'd faced in the jungles of New Britain. About four o'clock we halted to dig in for the night. The ground was soft, perfect for foxholes and setting up the mortars. I sent a couple of the men to check out a nearby farmhouse and they came back to report it clear.

Tex Cummings and I had just started to dig a foxhole when we heard the distant buzz of airplanes. We looked up and spotted two of them, just specks, but low and coming from the bay.

As we watched, the specks grew larger. They were going to fly close by.

"Well, here come two of ours," Tex said. "They're looking out for us."

I spotted the red circles on the sides of the planes. Meatballs we called them. You learned to recognize them instantly, a warning like the red hourglass on a spider.

"Better take another damn look, son," I said. "Those are Jap planes. They're probably spotting us."

They passed thirty or forty yards off, almost at eye level, and as they passed the pilots turned and looked right at us. It was one of those moments when time seems to stop, and I could clearly see every detail—their jackets, leather helmets, goggles up on their foreheads, white scarves. Then they roared on without swerving or changing course.

We stood waiting until they were gone. "Probably looking for bigger stuff," I said.

Neither of us had bothered to reach for our M1. We'd have to have been very, very lucky to hit one.

From where we dug in, we had a distant view of the invasion ships riding at anchor out in the bay. A little after our encounter with the two Zeros, another Jap plane passed high overhead, flying west toward the beach. Antiaircraft guns started banging away. We watched him calmly circle, like a hawk or a buzzard. As I stood there, I heard myself saying, "Somebody hit that son of a bitch! Somebody hit that son of a bitch."

Then he pointed his nose down and went into a steep dive, smacking one of our transports midship. Flame and smoke boiled up and the ship burned late into the evening. It was the first successful kamikaze attack I'd witnessed.

After sunset, the temperature slipped into the sixties and we pulled on our wool-lined jackets. We broke out the little bottles of brandy that were supposed to keep us warm. A breeze had carried off the haze and one by one the early stars came out. We settled in, sharing foxholes, one sleeping while the other stood watch.

Pretty soon somebody started scratching. Then somebody else

joined in. Then we were all scratching. We had bedded down in a nest of fleas, and they were having a feast at our expense. All night they kept after us, and you'd hear men flopping around, scratching and cursing. Still, I thought fleas were a better deal than Japs. First day of the invasion and none of us hurt or wounded. No artillery or mortar shells rained down on our heads. No banzai attacks. We kept asking ourselves, where were the Japs? Gradually, those whose turn it was to sleep drifted off into an uneasy rest.

Late at night the rattle of a tommy gun jerked us awake. Everybody popped up, alert. We shouted back and forth, "Everybody all right? What happened? Who's firing?"

Gene Sledge whispered that he was sure he'd spotted a Jap crouching over by a row of trees. Just to make sure he'd fired off a burst from the submachine gun. He didn't know if he'd hit anything.

Now, we were all on edge, waiting in silence and squinting into the darkness, trying to see whatever Sledge had seen. We strained, listening for groans, half expecting any minute to hear cries of *banzai!* Minutes went by with only an occasional pop and rumble in the far distance as some other unit dealt with its own troubles. Finally, those of us who were scheduled to sleep curled up in our foxholes again. The rest went on watching and listening.

At first light Sledge and a couple others walked over to the row of trees to see what, if anything, he'd hit. His Jap infiltrator turned out to be a small haystack that, seen from a certain angle in the darkness, just might have looked like a crouching man, at least to a nervous Marine.

We gave Sledgehammer hell all the rest of that day.

———————————

The First and Sixth divisions reached the east coast by afternoon on the third day, almost ten days ahead of schedule. We looked out across an area of marshes and freshwater ponds to Chimu Wan Bay and the East China Sea. Behind us, both airfields had been secured and the Seabees were starting to patch up the runways. Within a few more days squadrons of Marine Corsairs would settle in at both fields. Word was passed along that losses since the April 1 landing had been minimal—of the sixty thousand troops who came ashore, twenty-eight were killed, 104 wounded and twenty-seven missing.

The next morning it started to rain, and it would rain off and on for days after that, turning the roads to mud and slowing the flow of supplies. The Sixth Division turned north and the First Division got the order to move inland and probe the country to the southwest. K Company would spend the next week or so on patrol, looking for the enemy. While we didn't turn up a living Jap anywhere, to our north a patrol sent out by the Third Battalion of the Seventh Marines—also K Company, incidentally—ran into an ambush near a place called Hizoanna. Three of their men were killed and a dozen wounded in the firefight.

Within a few days we were ordered to patrol the same area. In the

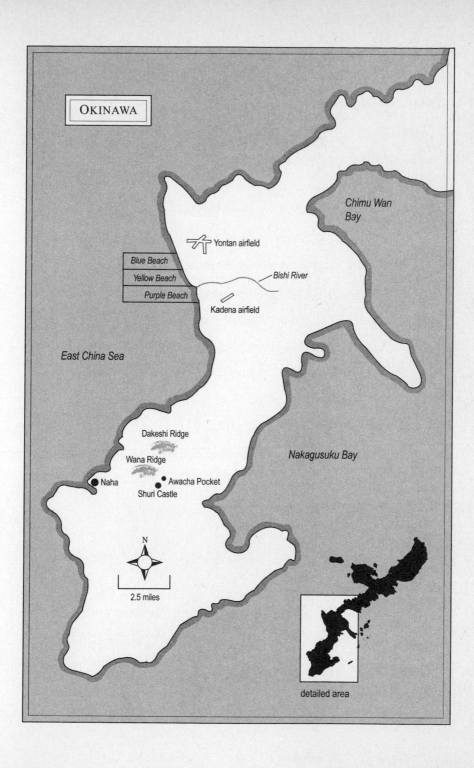

OKINAWA

Chimu Wan
Bay

Yontan airfield

Blue Beach

Yellow Beach   Bishi River

Purple Beach

Kadena airfield

East China Sea

Dakeshi Ridge

Wana Ridge   Nakagusuku Bay

Naha   Awacha Pocket
        Shuri Castle

N

2.5 miles

detailed area

morning, the section set out with Scotty in charge. The rain had let up and the road was dry, so we made good time moving along between rows of fragrant pine trees. But soon we passed the first sign of the Seventh Marines' scrape. A dead Jap was sprawled in a wooded ravine beside the road. A little farther along we came upon bloodied bandages and wrappings, and knapsacks that corpsmen had cut from injured Marines. There were about twenty more Jap bodies scattered around, along with empty ammo boxes and clips and lots of brass. Dark clots of blood soiled the ground. This had been more than a skirmish. We were all sharply reminded, if any of us needed reminding, that we were on Japanese soil. We were still in a war that could turn bloody any minute.

I sent a couple men forward to check the road where it dipped into a deep, tree-shaded cut. Scotty, our lieutenant, had wandered off into a nearby farmyard.

There was a shot, a pause, then another shot. Everyone dove for cover. The shots had come from the farmyard, not from the road, and my first thought was that Scotty had run into trouble.

I rose up to get a better look and spotted Scotty calmly standing in the open, taking aim with his carbine at the carcass of some dead animal. Just then he fired again.

I had no idea what the man was doing. But I knew it couldn't be very helpful. We picked ourselves up and gathered around while he cheerfully explained that he was trying to shoot the teeth out of the skull one by one. A regular shooting gallery.

Suddenly I was furious. The rest of the patrol standing around, white-faced, looked from me to Scotty and back to me again.

I decided to take him aside where we wouldn't be overheard.

"Lieutenant, what the hell did you think you were doing?" I said. "Now every Jap in ten miles is going to know exactly where we're at."

He looked down and shuffled his feet.

"You're responsible for the lives of twenty-two men here, and we're in the middle of God knows how many Japs. We don't need to hang up a billboard to tell them where to look for us."

He mumbled something about remaining alert while on patrol. I told him I didn't think being alert included taking target practice at dead animals.

It was a typical Scotty episode, the kind of dumb thing he'd probably think about later and come to regret. Scotty still had a lot to learn. I was doing my best to educate him.

He would give me another opportunity pretty soon after that.

Third Battalion got word to get ready to move out for another operation. Trucks drove us to the east coast, where amtracs waited on the shore. A cluster of five or six islands lay a few miles out in the bay, and while intelligence was pretty sure none of them harbored Japs, it was felt the enemy might use them in the future to launch a sneak attack.

While we waited to board the amtracs, we built a small fire to keep off the chill. Some of us were squaring away our gear when there was a familiar *pop!* About the time I'd made up my mind it was a grenade primer cap and everybody scattered for cover, there was a louder *pop!* and we were showered with ashes and sparks. A few grenade fragments landed among us, fortunately without doing any damage.

"Who's the stupid son of a bitch who pulled the pin on that grenade?" I yelled.

We all looked at Scotty, who was grinning sheepishly.

"Heh, heh. I guess I didn't get all the powder out of it," he said.

It was the old joke on maneuvers. Unscrew the detonator, pour the powder out of a grenade, screw the detonator back on, pull the pin and toss it to somebody. Everybody scatters, then everybody has a good laugh. But this time he hadn't poured out all the explosive charge, and we weren't laughing. And we weren't on maneuvers.

This time I didn't bother to take him aside.

"Well, how stupid can you get, Scotty?" I yelled at my section leader.

For once, he apologized.

We boarded the amtracs in a sour mood. Accompanied by a destroyer escort, they took K Company about four miles out to the largest of the islands, Takabanare. It didn't take us long to sweep the place, shore to shore. Whenever we came upon a house we'd check it out like a SWAT team, going from room to room with our pistols drawn. We turned up a few Okinawan natives but no enemy soldiers.

The first night Scotty and I dug in together. We took the split-bamboo mats the natives used for rugs and put them in the bottom of the foxhole to keep us dry. As it started to get dark, I noticed Scotty's .45 was still cocked.

"Scotty! Your pistol's cocked."

"God a-mighty," he said. "You know, I cocked that thing when we came ashore this morning, and never did uncock it."

For the next three nights we slept in the open. Our mortars were set up on a rocky hillside overlooking the beach, which was a fine place for swimming. A few swam out to the destroyer escort, which was anchored just offshore, and enjoyed the Navy's hospitality. Then, without explanation, the amtracs took us back to Okinawa, where we resumed our patrols.

With the Marine fighters onshore, things started getting interesting overhead. In my time overseas, I'd never seen planes tangle in dogfights before. On New Britain, there was so much jungle you couldn't see the sky most of the time, and during our time on Peleliu, the Japs had never been able to put a single plane into the air.

But on Okinawa the country was open, and we were close enough to Japan that they could fly in, fight, and then turn around and fly home. So we witnessed several dogfights, right over our heads. They were awesome.

Often they were so high you couldn't tell which planes were enemy and which were ours. They were just specks circling around up there. Then you'd see one get shot out of the air, and a wing would come spiraling down, or chunks of metal burning and trailing smoke. We'd just stand there staring upward.

On April 13, they passed the word along the lines that President Roosevelt had died the day before. It was a shock. Most of us hadn't spent much time thinking about events back home, what was going on in Washington and so forth. I guess we just assumed when we got back home he'd still be president. None of us knew a thing about this new man, Harry Truman.

I remember the day because that morning a Jap plane had come in low over our positions, treetop level. You could almost see his eyeballs. I thought, Oh, shit. He's after somebody. And just as I was thinking that, here came one of our Corsairs right on his tail. You could see the Marine pilot just as clearly. He was looking straight ahead, hunched over slightly. He hadn't started firing yet, but he was moving faster than the Zero. They disappeared behind the trees and I didn't get to see how it turned out. But I'd be willing to bet money that Marine caught him. And if he didn't catch him, somebody else did. Little by little we started to see fewer Jap planes.

Except for the dogfights, K Company had been on Okinawa almost a month now without seeing any combat. We'd been roaming the countryside, going out on patrol. Sometimes we'd just go out on our own, poking around farmhouses looking for chickens or pigs. Anything to relieve the monotony of K rations.

Toward the end of April I went out on my own to see what I could scare up. I came to this farmhouse with a shed built onto the side. The shed was about twenty feet long and six to eight feet deep with a door in front. It looked like the kind of place you might keep chickens, so I opened the door and went in. There was a ragged pile of pine limbs stacked near the door and I reached down and kind of shook one, hoping to scare up a chicken. And this man popped up instead.

You talk about West Texas quick-draw. The flap of my holster was down and snapped, but in one split second I had my .45 out and in that guy's face.

Then I saw that he was a civilian, an Okinawan. He just bowed, and bowed again and came out from behind the woodpile. I'm not sure which one of us was more startled. I patted him on the shoulder and bowed myself and left him standing there. I don't know where he went after that, whether he crawled back behind that woodpile or went somewhere else.

It was a nice farmhouse, wood frame, well kept. I don't think the Okinawans were happy to see us in the beginning. The Japs had kind of brainwashed them to think we were barbarians. But after they were in contact with us, word spread that we were okay. That we weren't the barbarians. The Japs were.

———

Our question—Where are the Japs?—finally had an answer.

Before we landed, most of them had been withdrawn to the southern third of the island, where they waited in caves and tunnels for us to come to them. Their guns were aimed and ready. It was the kind of last-ditch defense they had waged on Peleliu.

While the Marines were securing central and northern Okinawa, the Army's divisions started south. The farther south they got, the more opposition they ran into until they were fighting their way ridge to ridge. The Japs had established a defensive line across the island. On April 18, the Army staged a major attack. We sent an artillery regiment to support them. Then in a disastrous clash the Twenty-seventh Division lost twenty-two of its thirty tanks. The tanks and the supporting infantry had become separated, violating the cardinal rule of tank warfare. The attack stalled out and the First Marine Division's tanks had to be sent in as replacements. Then at the end of April the entire First Marine Division was ordered to replace the Twenty-seventh on the east end of the line. For the first time on Okinawa we were being thrown into battle.

On May 1 trucks took us south along muddy roads and across swollen streams. The thunder of artillery grew louder. We passed big guns and piles of empty shell casings.

For us Marines, the Twenty-seventh Division didn't have that great a reputation to begin with. They were a National Guard outfit from New York. On Saipan the division had failed to move forward during a Marine advance, and Marine General Holland "Howling Mad" Smith raised hell and got its commander replaced.

We piled out of the trucks in driving rain and started forward single file. Soon we encountered the sorriest bunch of soldiers coming our way I'd ever seen. They were what was left of the 106th Regiment of the Twenty-seventh Infantry Division, and they were exhausted, dead on their feet. In the days before, they'd fought their way to the top of the ridge and been thrown off. The next day they'd fought their way back up and been thrown off again. They were just getting the hell beat out of them when we relieved them.

As we were passing them, I witnessed an event that told me a lot about the outfit. One of their sergeants ordered a soldier to do something.

"Fuck you," the soldier snarled. "Do it yourself. I'm not doing it."

I don't recall what it was the sergeant ordered him to do. But I can sure tell you what would happen to a Marine who said that to his sergeant. He'd find himself toothless and in the brig. He didn't belong on the front line. There was no discipline whatever in the outfit, so far as I could tell. We thought they were the pits.

That day we fought our way to the top of that ridge. And we stayed there.

We got off the road and approached double time across an open field. Jap artillery had us zeroed in, or maybe they were firing at the 106th Regiment, which was still withdrawing. Shells were going off everywhere, and as we got closer, machine-gun and rifle fire joined in. The ground sloped upward, and we spread out to present a scattered target. Soldiers were still streaming by. It was the worst pounding we'd received since the airfield on Peleliu. Corpsmen were busy everywhere.

Just behind the crest of the ridge I yelled, "Hit the deck and dig in!" Our own guns were tossing shells across the top and, we hoped, into the Jap positions beyond.

We waited in our foxholes through the night, and the rain started up again, adding mud to all our other miseries. Word was passed along that next morning we'd begin moving southward, pushing the Japs back.

We awoke to a cold, gray dawn. Some of us tried to heat our coffee over a Sterno can. The rest huddled in their ponchos. At nine a.m. our artillery started firing across the ridge again, and the Japanese answered. But their shells were falling some distance behind us. I got word to start firing the mortars, and all along the line the tempo picked up. The rain also picked up, and Sledge and the other ammo carriers were slipping and sliding around in the mud, trying to get shells to the guns as fast as we could fire them. The Japs were somewhere on the far side of the ridgeline. I moved up front with the riflemen, where I could observe. But it was impossible to get a clear picture of what we were firing at. There were a couple of our snipers with me. Whenever they fired three or four shots, we'd have to move because Jap artillery would pick up on us.

Beyond our ridge lay a shallow valley, then another ridge. Whenever our men started to move forward, there was one particular Jap machine gun that would open up. Other enemy machine guns were firing that morning, but this one had us pinned down. He'd been waiting for us all night to cross the ridge and start down the other side.

Since I was head of the mortar section, it was now my job to clear a path so we could get moving again. And that machine gun was in our way.

Okinawa had these little mounds of dirt, maybe twenty or thirty feet across, scattered all over the southern part of the island, and one of them was right in front of us. It gave our riflemen some cover while they worked their way down the side, but as soon as they started off to the left, crouching down, that machine gun would start firing. Sometimes he'd let them get out a few yards into the open, then fire, like he was playing with them. We'd already had to lay down a screen of smoke grenades and send corpsmen after a couple wounded Marines.

Our three guns were about twenty-five or thirty yards behind me. I was communicating by phone. I could hear that machine chatter and I could hear the bullets zing by. I knew about where they were coming from, maybe four hundred yards across the valley and somewhere on our right. The valley was flat and open, but the opposite slope was thick with brush. I could not spot him to save my life.

I did notice one thing. The gunner would fire only after one of our men advanced past a certain point. I figured something had to be blocking his view. Since our men were headed toward the left, and away from him, when they moved out into the open they were looking in the wrong direction to see him. If I could get just past whatever was blocking his view of me, I'd get a clear view of him. I figured he'd likely fire at me just as he'd fired at everyone else that came along. But I'd see his muzzle flash. I'd know where that son of a bitch was.

The more I thought about it, the more sure I was that I could do it without getting hit, and if I could see him, I was confident we could take him out. I could land a mortar shell wherever I wanted to. That's one thing I could always do. I developed an eye hunting around the farm, shooting squirrels and, in fur-bearing season after a freeze, possums and coons and foxes. A man came to town on Saturdays and bought the pelts for a dollar or seventy-five cents each, something like that. I don't even know the first time I fired a gun, but I've hunted all my life. I still do.

But more than that, I think it came from Marine training, from hours of practice on the range and from competition between mortar squads. I could set up a mortar and get on target quicker than anybody.

I yelled at the section leader to hold his men while I tried something.

I started down and around the mound, slipping in the mud. Then, just before I got to where I judged I would be walking into the gunner's field of view, I turned and took a step or two backward, watching the distant ridge. Instantly I saw a flash on the far hillside. Mud spattered at my feet and I felt something whack my trouser legs. But I had seen him! I jumped for cover and grabbed the phone to call in the coordinates. Then I gave the command, "Fire!"

Now that I knew exactly where he was, I could observe the effect of our fire. The first round hit a few yards off to his left. I called in a correction—a couple degrees left, a few yards farther out—and I gave the fire command again. Seconds ticked by. There was a flash and a geyser of smoke and dirt. I watched that machine gun fly forward and the gunner do a kind of backflip through the air. I was sure we'd got two of them, since every gunner had a helper. We'd put that second shell right in their laps.

I thought, Boy, that's good shooting.

Then I looked down. There were three holes through my dungarees, two between my knee and ankle on the left, one just below my right knee.

But I was right. He hadn't hit me.

That put an end to it. The next day we went right on across the valley.

Our easy days on Okinawa were at an end. That's for sure.

Everybody sobered up now. Even Snafu Shelton turned serious. I would still have my differences with Scotty, even some serious differences. But our lieutenant seemed to mature as we went along. He lost his college kid silliness, and there was no more bragging about what he'd do to the Japs, no more pranks.

When I thought about it, I counted myself lucky to be serving with these men. We'd solidified into a unit. We worked well together. We had each other's backs.

I also counted myself lucky because I hadn't lost a man yet. Except for Redifer and Leslie Porter, who'd been nicked by that grenade at the pillbox on Ngesebus, my mortar squad hadn't even had anyone wounded. I felt lucky about myself. I had made six landings—Cape Gloucester, Talasea, Peleliu, Ngesebus, Okinawa, and Takabanare—and so far so good. Not that it couldn't happen to me. I saw guys around me all the time blown up, shot, cut down by shrapnel. I knew my time might come any minute.

It's just that it hadn't, so far.

CHAPTER 9

Flesh Wounds

Okinawa is a valley and a ridge, a valley and a ridge, all the way to the end of the island.

When I look at the map now, I see that we couldn't have been more than ten miles from the southern tip. But the Japs were going to make us fight for every inch of those ten miles. They had set up a defense line about three miles long across the island from the capital at Naha through an ancient fortress called Shuri Castle to Nakagusuku Bay. Their headquarters were in a big tunnel system beneath the castle, and their soldiers had been ordered to defend Shuri with their last drop of blood. North of the Shuri line they had set up their defenses on a series of parallel ridges—Awacha, Dakeshi and finally Wana. For the rest of May and into June we would throw ourselves against these ridges one by one.

When the rain let up the morning of May 3, we faced the first of those ridges. Scotty met with the company's commanders and then told me that the coming offensive would need the full support of our mortars. We got the section squared away and, as we fired out in front of them, K Company started across the valley. With that machine-gun nest cleared out, we made good progress. But the Japs stopped us short at the next ridgeline.

It was on this day, maybe the next, that two of my men were wounded. I was standing no more than ten feet away when the shell hit, and somehow I didn't get a scratch. But when the smoke and dust settled, both T. L. Hudson and Jim Kornaizl were down. Hudson's left arm was bloodied between the shoulder and elbow and he was holding it at an odd angle. Kornaizl was in the dirt, jerking from head to toe, his eyes rolled back. Our corpsman rushed over. A fragment had opened up the side of Kornaizl's skull. We got him out of there fast, then started patching up Hudson, whose arm was hanging uselessly.

Both would survive. Hudson would become my neighbor back in Texas for a time after the war was over. But I wouldn't see Kornaizl again for decades, and then I almost wouldn't recognize him. When I did, he would unlock a flood of memories.

That night our company got a needed rest. All night long we could hear heavy fire on our left, where the Japs staged a big counterattack. Far to the right, we could see tracers arc out over the bay where the First Marines were firing at Japs who were attempting a surprise landing behind our lines. If they had succeeded they might have rolled up the whole line. But the First caught them when they were still in the water, killing them by the hundreds before they even got to shore. The few stragglers that made it were hunted down the next morning.

During the night we were warned to watch for enemy paratroopers, but they never appeared. The Jap counterattack failed, and over the next few days we slowly began to fight our way forward again, taking heavy casualties. Our objective was a distant plateau, Dakeshi Ridge, overlooking the Awa River. From this and other ridges, the Japs had been able to fire down on our forces as they moved up along the coast.

On May 6 it started raining again, and for two days it never let up. Mud gummed up weapons everywhere along the line. Often we were setting up our mortars in a couple inches of water. Each time we fired, they sank deeper into the muck. We shored them up as best we could with boards and stones.

On May 8 we learned that the war had ended in Europe. Germany's surrender had come too late for J.D. and for a lot of other good men. But there were no signs the Japs would follow Germany's lead. For most of us, the end of fighting half a world away meant very little, except that maybe the flow of supplies would pick up and we'd get some help. But the Navy celebrated with a monster barrage that seemed to cut loose every gun on every ship within range of the Japs. If it did any good, you couldn't prove it by us. We were still catching hell.

The Sixth Marine Division moved in on our right and we moved farther in from the coast, to an area called the Awacha Pocket. Except for the rain and mud, the deep draws and steep hills reminded me of Peleliu. Once again the Japs had plenty of caves and dugouts to fire from. One position covered several others, and it was almost impossible to dig them out. The roads were impassable and even amtracs could not get through to where we were set up. So they dumped our supplies a couple hundred yards away on the far side of a shallow draw. If we wanted our supplies, we had to go get them.

The business of hauling ammo, rations and five-gallon water cans across that draw got to be almost more trouble than combat itself. It was all up-and-down work. The mud would build up on your boondockers, layer by layer, so if you weren't sinking down or sliding back into it you were tripping over yourself. To add to our troubles the Japs had discovered what we were up to and set up a Nambu machine gun at the head of that draw. Every Marine who crossed it drew fire.

I didn't see it, but at some point Redifer took it into his head to cover our men as they went across with smoke grenades. It didn't keep the machine gunner from firing but it spoiled his aim, and Sledge and a number of others got across safely.

Then Redifer spotted one of our tanks and ran after it. He got it stopped and pretty soon it came rumbling and clanking down into the draw, Redifer walking in front of it guiding it like one of those fellows that waves the planes into the ramp at the airport. He got the tank parked crossways in the draw, and our men resumed moving supplies across, crouching behind the tank as it rumbled back and forth. Redifer was directing all the way.

While this was going on First Lieutenant George Loveday showed up.

Loveday had taken over from Legs, the lieutenant I had several clashes with. I got along a lot better with Loveday, but he wasn't all that popular with the men. First, he just looked sloppy. His uniform never seemed to fit him right. Everything kind of hung out and dangled. A lot of the time he ran around wearing just his cloth cap, carrying his helmet tucked under his arm. When he got mad, which he did often, he'd rip off his cap and throw it down on the mud or dirt and stomp on it.

While Redifer was throwing smoke grenades, he had been standing on the side of the draw, out in the open. Loveday thought this made him an easy target, and he just reamed Redifer out, from one end to the other.

"You stupid son of a bitch," he yelled. "Don't you have any goddamn brains?"

Redifer just stood there in stunned silence. Then he walked off.

I don't think Loveday had seen the whole thing. He hadn't seen the trouble we were having getting supplies. I think what he saw was

Redifer exposing himself to enemy fire without taking any precautions. It might have been a dumb way to do it. But he did get the job done.

None of this meant either man was a bad Marine. Redifer was one of those guys who wasn't afraid of anything. He didn't always think first. But he was solid. Loveday had his faults. He had a temper. But hell, we've all got our faults. He was a good man, and a good officer. After World War II, he went on for a tour of duty in Korea and then to Vietnam.

Another major push against Awacha Pocket was set for noon on May 9. The rain slacked off, the ground was drying out and our tanks were on the scene. We resupplied with ammo and registered our mortars.

Once again there was a big bombardment before we kicked off. Artillery alternated with waves of swooping Avenger dive-bombers and Corsairs firing rockets. We called the rockets "Holy Moses," because we figured that's what anyone on the receiving end would say when they saw them coming. I was out front, observing and directing fire. I watched our riflemen and tanks start across the valley, only to be brought up short again by Jap fire. They were using their 90mm mortars, with big shells that made a strange fluttering sound as they came tumbling down. I ordered the mortars to fire phosphorous shells to provide a smoke screen for the attack.

At the end of the day we had made maybe a few hundred yards. Our battalion was relieved and went into reserve, with orders to back up the Seventh Regiment, who were fighting on our right on Dakeshi Ridge. The Seventh hammered at that ridge all night long and just before dawn we got word that we might be needed after all. We'd picked up some intelligence that the Japs might pull a counterattack. So we pulled up stakes and moved west along the ridge to where the attack was expected. There we found a group from First and Second battalions who had fought through the night hand to hand with the Japs. Here and there, corpsmen were patching up wounded Marines. A few yards beyond their foxholes, dozens of Japs were sprawled out in the mud. We'd missed the fight.

Minutes later we were ordered to turn around and go back to our old position.

After the Seventh Marines took Dakeshi Ridge, we moved into what was left of a small village just behind the ridge. Most of the buildings were down. But the low stone walls still stood along the roads, where they provided good cover. They were well made, about three or four feet high with large stones and mortar. I ordered everyone to dig in along the north side of the walls, where we'd be sheltered from fire.

That same night I got a look at one of the new night-vision scopes the Army was using. It took two or three guys to man that thing, but they could set it up after dark and see Jap infiltrators as they moved in, before they did their dirty work. One man held the scope and the other fired a BAR at the target. I looked through it. Everything had a strange, greenish glow, but I could see like daylight. I could recognize individuals thirty to fifty yards away, actually tell who they were.

I thought, Man alive! If you had one of these things when they came at you in a banzai charge, you wouldn't have to just fire into the dark and hope you'd hit one. You could pick them off like flies. I wondered how long until they were available for Marines.

About two o'clock in the morning, all hell broke loose over in one of our foxholes. I was only fifteen or twenty feet away and I recognized the voice. George Sarrett was yelling and thrashing around. I thought, God a-mighty! I've set us up where there's a Jap cave. They've come out and one of them is in the foxhole with George.

I scrambled over, pulling out my KA-BAR just as Sarrett stood up, panting and sputtering.

"Get him off me!" he yelled. "God, I hate those things!"

I looked down, expecting to find a bloodied Jap crumpled in the bottom of Sarrett's foxhole. Instead, there was a land crab that had tumbled in sometime during the night.

That crab gave us the first laugh we'd had in many weeks.

Beyond Dakeshi village we got held up at one particularly long, low ridge. Twice our men had made it almost to the top, only to be thrown back and pinned down in the valley. Each morning before they moved out, our artillery would raise hell, firing shell after shell over the crest. It wasn't doing a damn bit of good.

I watched from my forward position, directing the mortars, trying to figure out why artillery wasn't doing the job. It was passing over the ridgetop and exploding on the far side. It should be catching the Japs.

Something had to be running just beyond the crest that was sheltering them, something like a gully or a trench. The Japs could lay up in there protected from our artillery, then pop out and start firing when we moved up the slope.

The difference between artillery and mortar fire, as every Marine learns in boot camp, is that mortar fire drops down at a steep angle. You can't hide from it in a hole or a trench.

I called back to the mortars and explained to the men what I wanted.

"Register one gun to fire from right to left, the second to fire left to right, and the third to fire all along the crest of the ridge." Sledge, Shelton, Santos, Redifer, Sarrett and the others instantly got what I had in mind.

Scotty did not.

He came on the phone from the gun pits. "You can't do that!" he said. "We don't have enough ammo."

I'd had differences with Scotty before on setting up the mortars. I would be out on the line somewhere, and when I came back he would have them set up where they were subject to rifle fire from any angle. I'd have the guys move the guns to where at least they had some protection.

Then they'd have to re-dig all the foxholes. They didn't mind, because they knew that's where they should have set up to begin with. But nobody wanted to question Scotty's decisions. I had been through this a couple times already on Okinawa. Now I had to do it again.

I needed twenty rounds per gun, sixty shells in all, that I could throw at that thing. I knew damn well there had to be something there. I had them covered.

Scotty and I had a pretty good powwow over the phone. I tried to explain the situation and why my plan would work, but he didn't see it. Finally I thought, This is getting us nowhere. I called the company command post and explained what I wanted to do. "Can you spare us the ammo?" I asked.

"No problem," they said.

Scotty was back on the line, fuming. "I *order* you not to fire," he yelled.

I ignored him.

"Mortar section, fire on my command! Commence firing!"

Whatever Scotty had to say was drowned out in the *bump-bump-bump* of mortar fire.

Bill Sloan wrote in his book *The Ultimate Battle* that I told Scotty to go to hell. I want to clarify that. What I said was, "Scotty, if you're going to be so damned observing, get your ass up here on the front line where you can see what's going on."

That's exactly what I told him. But I didn't tell him to go to hell. He was my lieutenant.

K Company took the ridge without further trouble, and I didn't hear any more from Scotty. But when I got to the top I took a few minutes to look around. Sure enough, there was a narrow gully running right behind the crest. And laid out in the gully, almost side by side, I counted the bodies of more than fifty Japs.

We moved on, ridge to ridge, until we hardly knew anymore which was which. After days of shelling they were all as bare as plucked chickens. We moved along a narrow road between stone walls, always five paces apart. Keep moving! Don't bunch up! All the time we were working our way closer to Wana, the last ridge before Shuri Castle.

We were to relieve the First Marines, who had cut around the west end of the ridge and had been working their way east up Wana Draw. Three times they had been forced back under intense fire from the heights. Now they were exhausted. While the Seventh Marines concentrated on the ridge itself, to our left, we started fighting our way back up the draw, supported by tanks. The walls of that thing were two hundred feet high in places, and we saw more of the strange, horseshoe-shaped tombs the Okinawans carved out of solid rock. Whole families were buried in them, going back generations. The Okinawans considered them sacred ground. But the Japs fortified them and set up their antitank guns and mortars to fire down on us. They quickly knocked out two of our tanks and forced us back, but not before we were able to call in fire on two of their positions from the battleship *Colorado*.

Our Second Battalion managed to get a foothold on Hill 55, which anchored the west end of the draw. On the next morning, May 20, we started up Wana Draw again, making progress.

I felt a little uneasy that morning. It wasn't a feeling I could describe. As I said, I never for a moment believed I wouldn't come home from the war. But I was no fool. I knew that I could come home wounded or crippled.

The Japs started firing at us from the left, with a 150mm gun up on the ridge. Jim Burke and I were up front observing, and when those big shells started landing around us we thought we'd better get the hell out of Dodge. We ran down the slope to where there were a couple shell holes and Jim jumped into one and I tumbled into another. Just as I hit the bottom, there was a terrific *crack* just behind me, on the edge of that thing. I felt that force go right through me, and then dirt and rock come raining down. For a moment I couldn't see a thing, couldn't breathe. I was buried. I clawed my way out, caked with dirt, bruised and sputtering. I don't remember being relieved, thinking I'd had a close call. As a matter of fact, I don't remember much from the rest of that morning.

That afternoon about two o'clock we were sitting somewhere nearby, out in the open. That big ridge was still right in front of us and Marine and Navy planes were working it over, strafing and dropping bombs. Artillery was going on both sides. We were in the middle of it.

For some reason our new corpsman, Wesley Katz, took it into his head at that moment to start praying. Doc Caswell, who had been with us since Peleliu, had been wounded a couple days earlier, during the push up Wana Draw with the tanks.

I had nothing against prayer. I'd prayed myself from time to time, always quickly and silently. But Doc Katz was praying loudly. You could hear him over the roar of the airplanes and the rattle of shells. I reached over and patted him on the shoulder and said, in a soft voice, "Let's just have a silent prayer here, son. It's not doing the other troops any good."

He bowed his head and finished his prayer in silence.

A short time later I was sitting on my helmet eating ham and lima beans from a can when a big shell smacked down maybe fifty or a hundred yards away. Just a flash and a *crack!* The impact knocked me off my helmet and at the same time I felt something sting the back of my neck.

I sat on the ground for a moment, then reached up to brush away whatever was on my neck. I felt something hard and sharp, and this chunk of metal fell on the ground. It was about as long and as big around as my finger, tapered and real jagged. I reached down to pick it up but it was hot and I dropped it. I waited a second and picked it up again. I looked at it and put it into my pocket. I felt blood trickle down my neck.

Katz was at my side. He started dressing the wound. It had been numb but now it was starting to really hurt. Three or four minutes had gone by. Doc poked me with a syrette. I stood up and turned my neck just to make sure everything still worked. Nothing was broken.

"Do you think you can walk?" Katz asked.

I felt a little light-headed, but I thought I knew where I was. I nodded and he pointed the way to the first aid station, a few hundred yards off. I stumbled in that direction with the battle still going on all around me, bullets singing and shells falling. I don't know how the heck I made it, but I did.

I stayed at the first aid station until it started to get dark. Then a jeep ambulance came and took several of us to the forward field hospital. I remember on the ambulance holding a plasma bottle for a guy who really was in a bad way, but I don't remember much else. I'm sure he was dying.

The field hospital was little more than a big tent with stretchers on the bare ground. They brought me in and I lay down on one of the stretchers. An Army medic eventually came by and gave me a couple of shots. I thought, That's good. That's for the pain and for tetanus. After a while, another corpsman came by and gave me another shot. A little while later, I got one more shot.

When I looked up again, there was another medic standing there. He said he was going to give me a shot.

"Hell, I've already had three shots," I said. "What's going on?"

He stared at me. "You've had three shots already?"

"Hell, yes. I've already had three. And now you're wanting to give me a fourth."

He stood there a moment. Then he shook his head and walked away.

The next morning they picked me up on a stretcher and put me in an ambulance and took me to another hospital, farther from the front. It was a tent, but it had a floor and real doctors and nurses. I was lying in a bed. For some reason my whole abdomen hurt. A nurse came by and said she was going to give me a sponge bath. I told her about the pain.

"Let's see what the problem is."

She pulled back the covers and started to sponge me gently. My stomach was so sore I could hardly stand to be touched.

"Have you been close to an exploding shell?" she asked.

I remembered diving into the crater just as the 150mm shell went off, and being buried in dirt.

"Yes, ma'am. Artillery shell yesterday morning, just about as close as you can get and still be here."

"You've had a concussion," she said. "That's your problem. A couple days will take care of it."

She sponged me gently, and the dirt and dead skin came rolling off. You never realize in combat just how filthy you get. But I won't ever forget her tenderness and kindness. She gave me some pills for the pain, and three or four days later it eased up, just as she said.

As soon as I was able I got some Red Cross stationery and wrote to Florence.

"Just a few lines to let you know I was hit Sunday May 20th, but don't worry, Darling, I am not suffering & haven't been at all."

I told her I'd just been scratched, no serious damage done, which was mostly true.

Now that I was out of combat, I found myself thinking about her almost all the time.

"I sure wish I had you here, Darling, to change the bandages & give me about a million sweet kisses a day or more. I am sleeping on nice white sheets with the softest pillow. It sure beats a wet foxhole."

They showed a movie to some of us who could get around, *In Old Oklahoma*, with John Wayne and Gabby Hayes. I was able to relax and enjoy it.

I don't remember that they ever stitched me up. I think they just let the skin grow back over the wound. There was no infection. I had been lucky.

A doctor came in every morning to make his rounds. My cot was the second or third one on the right. After he'd seen everybody else, he'd stop and sit on my bunk and we'd talk for ten or fifteen minutes.

It turned out he was from San Antonio, so we hit it off right away. All through the war, it was that way whenever I ran into someone from Texas, an instant bond. We were buddies.

Doc Moore was his name. He told me I had been very lucky.

"Why is that?"

"If that fragment had gone any deeper it would have hit your thyroid."

"Would that be bad?"

He showed me where my thyroid gland was located, right behind the voice box, and explained how the thyroid affected everything from digestion to energy level. A damaged thyroid could affect me in several ways, he said.

"You might become real, real thin. Or you could become grossly obese. Either way, it would have messed you up for life."

So I guessed I was luckier than I thought.

Pretty soon I started feeling restless and eager to get back to K Company. I had written Florence a couple more letters, but I didn't get any replies. In fact, I hadn't received mail from anybody while I was in the hospital, so I figured the mail system had screwed up and lost track of me. On June 9 Doc Moore gave me a clean bill of health and the hospital turned me loose. It had been twenty days since I'd been wounded. I asked around if anybody knew the location of Third Battalion's K Company, and the next day I hitched rides on Army trucks headed south toward the front.

In my pocket I still carried the shell fragment that had cost me so much trouble.

═══════════

Gene Sledge described the fight for Shuri Castle as a time of "mud and maggots." The rains started up again the day after I was wounded and went on for the next ten days without a letup. I could hear them drumming on the roof of the hospital, but I had no idea how bad it was out on the battle line.

For K Company these were some of the worst days of the war. The fighting was so intense that neither side had time to gather its dead, which were left to rot in the mud on the battlefield. Maggots were everywhere. If a man slipped in the mud, he stood up covered with maggots. They filled his pockets. The Japs were shelling anything that moved, and the sheer noise and force of the explosions left men dazed and deaf. Stumpy Stanley, our company commander, came down with malaria. He was so delirious he refused to leave his command post until a corpsman dragged him to a first aid station. Lieutenant Loveday took his place.

On May 29, while I was on the road to recovery, Companies L, K, and I captured the area around Shuri Castle and flew a Confederate flag from the ramparts. Most of the Japs fled south. First Regiment relieved the Fifth Marines on June 4. The next day the rains ended.

I found my old company several miles south of where I'd left them.

We were in a bad way. We'd lost thirty-six men in the fighting around Shuri Castle and we were down to about a hundred enlisted men and three or four officers. The word was that the Fifth Regiment would not be sent into combat again.

Because the rains had gummed up the roads, the Navy had been air-dropping food, water and ammo from TBM Avenger dive-bombers. Somebody found a cache of Jap rations. Everything was in cans. I ate some of their tuna fish and mandarins, little orange sections. It wasn't too bad. We ran across saki quite often. A lot of the guys drank it. I couldn't stand the taste.

Most of the time we were going out on patrol, sealing caves and trying to find pockets of Jap stragglers. The Japs had been squeezed into an area maybe three miles long by four miles wide, their backs were to the coastline. There was no place else to go.

We'd been warned not to go into the caves, but I got curious. I put a Sterno can on the end of a stick, like a candle, and felt my way down into one cave we had come across. You couldn't see three feet in front of you. Some distance inside I came upon a cot. I put my hand down to feel it and it was still warm.

I stopped, listening. Somewhere close by I could hear a clock ticking. I thought, Burgin, get the hell out of here. When you're in a cave looking out, you can see anything between you and the opening as plain as day. But if you're looking in, you can't see a thing, even holding a little Sterno candle in front of you. So I started backing out very slowly. Thank God, I didn't get killed. When I got outside, I called the demolition people, and they sealed up the whole thing with a satchel charge.

I'm sure to this day there was a Jap inside there, because that cot was warm. Why didn't he shoot me? Maybe he didn't want to draw attention to himself. Maybe he thought he could sneak out at night and do more damage than by just killing one Marine. I don't know. He sure as hell had the opportunity.

I swore then and there that I'd never go into another cave.

There were caves everywhere, most of them full of Japs. The First and Seventh Marines had fought their way to the top of the last ridge before the coast, Kunishi Ridge. But the Japs were inside, fighting from caves, and the men on top were cut off from supplies and reinforcements. We knew both regiments were suffering heavy losses. On June 14 we were ordered to square away our equipment and get ready to move south the next morning. None of us was very happy about this development, but it was the only way.

Along with tanks and amtracs, we moved out single file on both sides of a dusty road. The noise of the battle grew louder and we saw more and more ambulance jeeps headed north full of wounded Marines, not a good sign. We came to a broad, open area of rice paddies with a long, steep ridge rising up beyond. For those of us who had fought on Peleliu, it reminded us of Bloody Nose Ridge, where we'd been exposed to such devastating fire from above.

We dug in for the night alongside the road and the next morning started toward a hill a mile or so to our left. We were moving along in a column when I heard the *snap* of a Jap rifle and felt a bullet pass by my ear. It was so close I could literally feel the heat. I didn't stop, I didn't pause, I didn't even duck. I just kept walking at the same pace, thinking, Those sons of bitches are still trying to kill me.

Somebody else back in the line might have seen the shooter and picked him off. Maybe he didn't fire again. I don't know. By then I think I was pretty much running on automatic pilot.

———————

We knew Kunishi Ridge would be our last big fight. Mostly it was a rifleman's fight, up the slope cave by cave and sniper by sniper. The Japs fired back with everything they had. Corpsmen started bringing our wounded down almost immediately. Because our men were working their way up the ridge, we couldn't risk mortar fire, so the section was posted at the bottom to watch for infiltrators who might try to work their way around and come in from the east. When needed, we acted as stretcher bearers.

The worst of it was June 18. A sniper shot Tex Cummings, one of the two ammo carriers I'd picked up for the squad on Pavuvu. The bullet hit him in the back and passed clean through, collapsing his lung. We called in an amtrac and loaded him on board as quick as we could. Then a grenade from a knee mortar went off beside Harry Bender, our

BAR man. We carried him out with fragments in both legs, his back and his head. That same day we got word that Lieutenant General Simon Bolivar Buckner, commander of the entire invasion, had been killed by a Jap artillery shell while he was observing the Eighth Marines on the far west end of the line. Buckner was the son of a Confederate general and the highest ranking U.S. military officer killed during World War II. One of our own, Lieutenant General Roy Geiger, took over the Tenth Army. Geiger had been with us on Peleliu. It was the first time ever that a Marine general was placed in command of a standing army.

In the two days of fighting on Kunishi Ridge, K Company lost thirty-three men, five of them killed. Every casualty now was a painful reminder that even though the Japs were down to their last caves and the battle for Okinawa was almost over, any one of us could still go home wounded or crippled for life, or in a coffin. We were all thinking the same thing: If Okinawa was this bad, how bloody was it going to be fighting the Japs on their home ground? We knew we would soon have that to face.

Late on June 18, the Eighth Marines relieved us and we came off the ridge. The Eighth had fought on Tarawa and Saipan, and looked fit and fresh. As we moved off south along the road, Jap artillery was still raining down on our tanks and amtracs, and occasionally knocking one out. But more and more their fire came from isolated positions. By the afternoon of June 20 we could finally look out over the sea. Whatever

Japs were left by now were dug in behind us. It was only a matter of rooting them out of their hiding places. And they still prowled by night. Some of them got through our lines and we could see them wading out in the surf, where they made excellent targets.

The next day, whoever made such decisions declared Okinawa officially secured. Our mail caught up with us and with it was a packet of letters from Florence. She hadn't heard from me since I had been wounded, and she was worried. I sat down to reassure her right away.

I told her I was out of the hospital, feeling "fine and dandy."

"Guess what, Darling? The Navy just gave us an orange and four eggs apiece. Boy do they look good after looking at C rations ever since April the first."

Then I got down to what had been on my mind.

"I wish that we would have got married when I was there, and now you would be going to the States this month. . . . Why didn't you drag me to the altar when I was there and marry me? Darling, I sure hope it won't be long until you can come to me & the war is over so we can cuddle in a little home of our own."

I was pretty sure that I would soon be heading home. Florence had been working on her end at getting all the papers she would need to move to the States. I would soon start filling out the necessary paper-work on my end. I promised to cable her as soon as I had any news.

We were sent out on burial details, shoveling dirt over enemy dead, and gathering up spent brass from the battlefield. We went hunting for

Japs still holed up in caves and large Okinawan family tombs. A few of them were even surrendering, which was something we'd never seen before. I watched one small group creep out of a cave, no more than three or four of them. They were wearing only their jock straps, and one was carrying a white flag.

When they wouldn't surrender, we'd call up flamethrower tanks or have the demolition men blast the entrance shut. Many of their officers, we heard, committed ritual suicide. On the morning of June 22 after an all-night banquet with their staff, the Japanese commander, Lieutenant General Mitsuru Ushijima, and his aide, Major General Isamu Cho, killed themselves on a ledge overlooking the ocean. They had ordered their soldiers to carry on the fight to the last man, which for some of our troops meant at least another month of fighting. But the Fifth Marines were to be sent north, out of the battle at last.

We needed a rest. We'd been on Okinawa now for three months, in combat continuously for two months. Everybody's nerves were shot. Everybody was on edge.

They had set up a mess hall in a tent. You stood up to eat, at tables that were about four feet high. One day we were having soup for lunch. Private First Class David Burton Augustus Salsby was standing straight across from me. The table wasn't that wide, maybe two feet.

Salsby was from Idaho, a little guy about five feet four, and he had that Little Man Syndrome. He'd been wounded and returned to duty, and he was cocky. He thought no harm could come to him. He was also tough. He could do anything anyone else could do.

Each time he raised his spoon to his mouth he'd slurp. Real loud. *Slurp! Slurp!*

"Salsby, don't do that," I finally said. "That just rakes my nerves over when you do that."

He looked up at me.

"Burgin, you can tell me what to do when we're on duty. But whenever I'm off duty I'll do as I damn please."

I reached across and grabbed his lapels and lifted him right off the floor and pulled him up close to my face.

"You little son of a bitch! If you do that one more time I'll knock your damn teeth out. Do we understand each other?"

I set him down. He didn't slurp anymore. It shows the frame of mind we were all in by then.

Okinawa had one more little surprise for us, before we headed north.

I was sitting there when something caused me to look up. I saw the ground rolling toward me like an ocean wave. The wave just lifted me and then went on by and that was that. While it was happening the strangest feeling came over me. Like nothing in the world was steady or solid. It was over with that quick, but I'll never forget that feeling. We had had a little earthquake, the first I'd ever experienced.

The trucks picked us up early in July and we rode north through a landscape that we could hardly recognize. The Seabees and construction crews were at work everywhere. Roads were being surfaced with crushed coral, huge stockpiles of supplies were being built up. Planes were flying in and out of the airfields constantly. Okinawa was being transformed into a base for the invasion of Japan.

The enlisted men settled into a camp on Motubu, a large peninsula just north of the beaches where we had landed on April 1. NCOs were driven farther north almost to the tip of the island, where a camp was already set up. Tents were in place, roads surfaced. A short runway for the spotter planes ran through the center of the camp.

It's a funny thing, but I don't remember much about that camp. I can't remember where the chow hall was, where the heads were. The two most important places in camp. I can remember where the doctor's office was. But there's just so many things that I can't recall. I guess I was just wiped out by then. I think from thirty months of combat, from losing men from my platoon, guys that I had known since Melbourne, guys that were gone. Hillbilly Jones, Captain Haldane, and the others. I was pretty stressed out, no doubt. Just flat numb.

I slept with Florence's picture under my pillow, and thought of the days when we would have a home of our own, and children to call us Mother and Dad. I was sure I had accumulated enough points to be rotated back to the States. The problem was, Florence was in Melbourne. Our plans were to make a home together in Texas, and I was trying to work it out. Thousands of American servicemen had married Australians. When travel was possible again, wives with children would get first priority to go to the States. After that would come wives without children. Only after they'd been accommodated would fiancées be allowed to travel.

"I just talked to my company commander about the papers," I wrote her in mid-July, "and he is going to see about them in the morning. I hope I can get them fixed up before I go home. Oh how I hope & pray I can. I want to have your name on the list, knowing it won't be too long before you can come home to me forever, Darling, & I do mean forever."

Some of the guys were being married by proxy, and Florence and I had talked about it in our letters. But when it came down to it, I didn't want to get married that way. I wanted a real wedding in a church and a real life again.

We hadn't seen each other in almost two years. I could tell from her letters she was as anxious as I was. And she still worried about my wound.

"Really, Darling, it didn't hurt me," I wrote her. "I hardly have a scar to show for it. I have been hurt a lot worse in a football game, and never stopped playing."

I have no memory of hearing about the atomic bomb. I guess I heard about it on Armed Forces Radio. Of course, I didn't know what an atomic bomb was, so it didn't mean a whole lot to me. They said it did terrible damage, but that's about all we knew. A week or so later we got word that the Japs had surrendered. It was over, and that was a good feeling. We knew we'd be going home, though we didn't know when. But there wasn't a lot of hooting and hollering, no big celebration. The folks back in the States probably celebrated more than we did.

I did see one Marine celebrate. The day the war ended or the next, a Corsair came buzzing down our little runway, upside down all the way. The pilot could have opened his canopy, stuck out his hand and dragged his fingers along the ground. That's how low he was. I just knew he was going to crash, but he flew on down the runway, pointed the nose of that Corsair up and flew straight up into the air. Then he turned around, did a nosedive, flipped that plane over again and made the trip back down the runway in the opposite direction, upside down all the way again. He pulled up and ended with several rolls, then flew off.

I stood there gawking, as I had back in boot camp when those fighters came roaring off the runway at North Island. I thought, You crazy son of a bitch. You're going to crash. Those Marine pilots, they were good. They were something else.

I had nothing to do now but wait. The sergeants were all bunking together. I was still in charge of the mortar section, but they were bunking down the street. If I needed anybody to do anything, I just hollered. I was tired, but my wound had healed. Then one day I suddenly felt a chill. Within minutes I was shivering violently. I couldn't seem to get warm. The feeling passed but a short time later I started sweating. I was burning up with fever. I went down to the camp doctor's office, my knees so wobbly I could hardly walk.

I knew very well what it was. I'd seen it often enough in others. Like so many Marines, I'd come down with malaria. The doctor started me on quinine and increased the Atabrine tablets I'd been taking, like everyone else. I went back to my tent to lie down, alternately shivering and sweating for the rest of the day. All week I lay in my cot or, when I felt strong enough, got up and wandered around a bit. The fevers and chills gradually lessened. But the truth of it is, you never really get over malaria. The symptoms go away. But months and even years later they can come back. Malaria was to be an off-and-on presence in my life for some time to come.

It was September 14 before I finally learned I was being shipped back to the States. The rest of the First Marine Division were going to China. The next day I went down to the enlisted men's camp and looked for my old buddies. I spent most of the day going from tent to tent saying my good-byes. Some were already on board ship. Late in the month the First Marine Division left Okinawa for China. Jim Burke, Sledgehammer, Hank Boyes, Snafu Shelton, Sarrett, Santos—the guys I'd fought alongside, all my old buddies—were gone. I was on my own.

In the weeks afterward I moved from the NCO camp to another camp, where I sat through a raging typhoon. When it was safe to go outside the first thing I saw was a cargo ship blown right up onto dry land. It was a foretaste of what the sea can do. After the typhoon I moved closer to the harbor, with the Eleventh Artillery Regiment, where I bunked until it was time to ship out.

The eighty-two-day battle for Okinawa had taken more than twelve thousand American lives, and left more than thirty-eight thousand wounded. Nobody has ever been able to calculate exactly how many Japanese soldiers and Okinawan civilians died in that campaign. Even after the surrender, small pockets of Japs went on fighting, just as they had on Peleliu.

CHAPTER 10

Home Port

I came off watch on the pitching deck of the USS *Lavaca* at midnight and felt my way down the ladder to the cramped sleeping quarters. It had been a rough night with the ship bucking heavy seas. The air below was close and foul as I squeezed between the tiers of bunks filled with snoring men. I found my own bunk, shed my dripping poncho and threw myself down. I closed my eyes in relief. One more day closer to home.

It certainly hadn't turned into any bon voyage.

I had witnessed what a typhoon could do the week before on Okinawa, when a storm parked a ship on dry land, practically at the doorstep of my tent. That morning I went out and walked around. It looked like a good old Texas tornado had passed through. Two-by-fours were driven slantwise into the ground, trees uprooted and tipped over, roofs peeled away in ragged strips. The transport that was to take the Fifth Marines to China had sailed out of the harbor to weather the typhoon at sea, rather than risk being driven aground.

Just before I left the island I hooked up with another Texan, Ernest Schelgren, a platoon sergeant in the Eleventh Artillery who was also awaiting shipment home. He was from a farm and I was from a farm, and we hit it off. On October 16 we boarded the USS *Lavaca* together, looking forward to calm seas and an uneventful voyage. A few days out a typhoon caught us.

The *Lavaca* was an attack transport, built just a few years before but already a bucket of rust, a real tub. A couple days out I got assigned to guard duty on deck for four hours. As we watched clouds pile up across our path, the skipper came on the loudspeaker warning the crew to batten down the hatches. Everyone was ordered to wear life jackets and to stay below. Except those of us unlucky enough to be on watch.

Topside, I clipped on to the fore and aft line, a rope three or four inches thick that ran from the bow to the stern. It was the only thing you could hang on to.

The wind strummed the wires and the *Lavaca* creaked and groaned. Spray washed over the deck, and, as we got deeper into the storm, raging rivers of foam five and six feet deep. A crewman said the waves were fifty feet high, and I believed every word. They were taller than the ship. The *Lavaca* would climb up one side of a wave, seeming to take forever. Then it would tip, slide down the other side and start the long climb up again. It was a little like fighting across the ridges and valleys of Okinawa.

When I got below after my watch, the bunks were swinging against the sway of the ship. In bed at last, I adjusted my arms and legs, stretched out and closed my eyes. Maybe I even drifted off to sleep for a minute or two. Suddenly there was a roaring grind like metal being torn from metal, and a *bang!* I bolted up, wide-awake. We were next to the ship's galley and I could guess what had happened. In all the tossing and heaving, a stove had torn loose from its moorings and come sliding across the floor and slammed into the bulkhead. Now with a complaining screech it started sliding back the other way. Canteens and canteen cups, shaving kits and mess kits were clattering on the deck, tumbling off the overhead beams where owners had left them for safekeeping. In the semidarkness there were groans and shouts of alarm.

I thought, Well, it'd be a helluva time to have your ship go under and drown, on your way home. Then I thought, I'll just lie here and I'll find out right quick if we're still afloat or not. The ship went up, then it came down. Then it went up again, each time about fifty feet, and it came down. I decided, Okay, we're still afloat.

So I turned over and went to sleep.

The storm went on for seventeen hours, during which nobody

moved around much. A lot of the guys got seasick, which made the smell in the hold even worse. I didn't get seasick but a few days after we passed through the storm, my chills and fevers returned. I was sent to sick bay with malaria.

After three weeks at sea we sailed past the Golden Gate Bridge and the Oakland Bay Bridge one morning and docked in San Francisco. None of us went ashore. Before the end of the day we were on our way again, down the coast to San Diego.

I was feeling reasonably like a human being again. The Red Cross met us at the dock with paper cups of orange juice and half pints of milk. Trucks were waiting, engines running. The Navy had taken over Camp Elliott, where I had departed for the war thirty-two months before, so we were driven to Camp Pendleton. I'll never forget the first night in the barracks. The weather wasn't freezing, it wasn't even particularly cold. But I was the coldest I'd ever been in my life. After so many months in the southwest Pacific I guess my blood was thin.

I had an upper bunk. There was a mattress, a pillow, a sheet and one thin blanket. Between the mattress and the springs was a cloth pad, a mattress protector. After a few hours, I climbed out of bed and put my clothes on. I crawled back under that blanket but I was still freezing to death. Literally shaking. I thought, To hell with this, and I pulled the mattress over me, and that's where I spent the night, sleeping on that mattress pad. I never did get warm until I got up next morning.

While we waited to be mustered out, Ernest Schelgren and I hung out together. His wife, Barbara, flew in from Dallas to meet him and we became good friends, and remained so for many years after. My sister Ila was sending me money so I was able to go out on the town whenever I got liberty.

It took the Marines almost a month to return me to civilian life. I turned in my equipment, filled out lots of papers and sat through a final interview. I was surprised that the interviewer didn't ask whether I had been wounded or whether I had any medical problems. When it was over the Marines paid for a train ticket back to Texas. I was in a hurry and I flew home instead.

I moved in with my sister Ila in Dallas, then took the train down to spend Christmas with my parents at Jewett. My father had set aside a calf for me, as he did for each of the Burgin children. But I didn't want to farm. I had seen him work too long and too hard for too little. In a month I returned to Dallas and started looking for a job. I had a pretty good idea of what I wanted to do with my life.

I had already started the paperwork on Okinawa to bring over Florence. Although I had never officially proposed to her, it was always understood between us that we were going to marry after the war. I had written to her father asking for her hand. She told me once in Melbourne that he threatened to shoot "that Yank" if I came around trying to date his daughter. We had a good laugh over that. He didn't even own a gun. Fortunately, he sent his permission.

I listed her as my fiancée, which meant she had to wait in line behind all the wives and the wives with children before she could come to the United States. Once the paperwork was approved I had to post $500 with the government. This was a technicality, in case a fiancée arrived in the United States and the couple ended up not getting married, or they got divorced quickly. Then the money would go to the young woman to pay for her passage home. If the couple married, the government would return the $500.

Neither one of us had any doubts. We longed for the day we would finally be together. I put us on the waiting list for a new refrigerator and started looking for an apartment—not an easy thing to find in the months after the war, when GIs were returning home by the tens of thousands.

I bought a '39 Plymouth to help me in my job search. Growing up in rural Texas I had admired the mail carriers. I knew both of the rural route carriers who worked out of Jewett. I had been in their homes. They were friendly men and they had decent jobs during the Depression. I always figured that someday I would work for the federal government, because that meant job security and a good retirement plan.

I went to the Veterans Administration to see the contact officer. He was a man named Frank Mallory and he took an interest in my case. I think he took an interest in all the returning vets, because he was that kind of person.

We were sitting in his office talking and I told him I wanted to work for the Post Office. I'd had another bout of malaria and red, itchy fever blisters had spread over my chin and nose. I couldn't have weighed more than 140 pounds.

"Are you drawing disability?" Mallory asked.

I wasn't.

"And they didn't ask you about it when you were discharged?"

I said they hadn't mentioned anything about malaria or any medical problems.

"Well, somebody wasn't doing his job," he said. "What we're going to do is put in for a pension and let you start drawing compensation for this."

He showed me how to fill out the papers and gave me an addressed and stamped envelope. He also arranged for me to get on the list for the Civil Service exam for the Post Office.

A month or so afterward I got a check for 60 percent disability pay retroactive to my discharge.

In February, T. L. Hudson showed up. He'd gotten over the wounds he'd received on Okinawa. We found a boardinghouse where we could bunk together and the rent included breakfast. We became very close friends.

That month, I was notified that I had been recommended for a Bronze Star for my role in wiping out the machine-gun nest on Okinawa. This was the first I'd heard, but welcome news. I went out and bought my first and only set of Marine dress blues for the presentation ceremony, which was held in Dallas's Oak Cliff YMCA. My dad and mother drove up from Jewett to stand beside their proud son, the only time they ever saw me in a Marine uniform.

When my health got to the point that I was able to go to work I decided to try the railroad company. They put me in telegraphy school for two months, but just before graduation I found out they planned to stick me in a little station way out just this side of El Paso. No town, no settlement of any kind, not even a gas station. Just a lonely railroad agency beside the track. I could imagine how Florence would take to that, and it wasn't what I'd had in mind either, so I said, No, thanks. With Mallory's help, I landed a job on the assembly line at the Ford plant in East Dallas. I worked there three months making $1.28 an hour—which was pretty good—when a letter came from the Post Office telling me to come in for the Civil Service exam.

I went to work for the Post Office on May 15, 1946, carrying the U.S. mail for eighty-four cents an hour, enduring the heat and fighting off mean dogs in East Dallas.

Back in Melbourne, Florence took the tram to the American consulate every Saturday, where she sat waiting patiently for the papers that would allow her to come to the United States. Women who had married American servicemen came and went, but there was nothing else either one of us could do but wait.

My sisters and mother were almost as eager as we were. They had been exchanging letters with Florence for more than a year. As soon as my mother found out we planned to marry, she wrote Florence that we were a simple farm family, not rich or glamorous. Florence wrote back that that was fine with her. She, too, came from a simple working-class family. After that, they hit it off just fine.

The year was almost over before we learned that the gate was finally open. In early January 1947, Florence said good-bye to her family and boarded a ship at Port Melbourne. There were five hundred passengers on board, and four hundred of them were the fiancées of American servicemen. I found us an apartment. It wasn't the little cottage I'd envisioned those hours daydreaming in tents and foxholes halfway around the world. But it was a start. I had a good job, and she was on her way. She managed the whole thing, lining up passage on the ship and a railroad ticket from San Francisco to Dallas, and wrote me to expect her the morning of January 27.

Riding east on the train she made friends with an older woman, also bound for Dallas. Florence told the woman how she met this American Marine in Australia, how love had triumphed and that she was headed to Dallas to marry him.

The woman looked doubtful.

"Are you sure he's going to be there at the station?"

"He'll be there."

As it turned out, I wasn't.

I got to the Dallas Union Station that morning in plenty of time for the train. But it wasn't the train she was on. I inquired when the next train would be in, then went back to the boardinghouse and had breakfast. I got back to the station fifteen minutes late for the next train and finally found Florence standing in the waiting room with her luggage, her new friend standing by her side in case I didn't show up. Florence looked just like I remembered her, only better. We hugged like any couple in love who haven't seen each other for years. The woman from the train disappeared. We never did get her name.

Florence had assumed we would be married on February 15, her twenty-first birthday. But we had an apartment. The refrigerator had been delivered. My family had even arranged for the church and a cake. And so on January 29, 1947, two days after she stepped off the train, three years and nine months after we met in Melbourne, my Australian bride and I were married in the Saner Avenue Church of Christ.

Though we had gotten off to a late start, we were like tens of thousands of other new couples in 1947, struggling to realize the American dream. Florence loved my family, and they loved her. She learned all my mother's favorite recipes and fit right in. Our oldest, Margaret Ann, was born that November. We lived in the apartment for a few more months—T. L. Hudson was our upstairs neighbor—and then bought our first house, a two-bedroom in a quiet neighborhood close in. Vicki Lynn came along in 1950, then Vanessa Jo in 1953. Florence always told her mom she was going to have eleven boys and one girl. When our fourth girl came along in 1955, we said, That's it, and gave her a boy's name, Terrie Lee. A few years later we bought a three-bedroom a little farther out. And in 1965, we built our dream house in the country, on a wooded tract overlooking a stream.

I put the war out of my mind and buckled down to work at the Post Office. In 1947 I had my last episode of malaria, which landed me in the veterans' hospital for a week. I got off the mail route that summer and became a postal clerk. A few years later I started studying for the supervisor's exam. I went from clerk to line foreman to general foreman to tour superintendent and finally to superintendent of registered mail. Each step of the way I found my old Marine experience stood me well. It was like being a section leader. As I moved from one supervisor's job to the next, I always made it my business to find out who were the natural leaders, the ones you could depend upon, and who were the troublemakers. And like my old San Diego drill instructors, I never had to yell at anyone to get anything done.

Three of our girls graduated from college. One went to a junior college. Florence and I became grandparents four times over. And then great-grandparents, three times so far. The girls are everything we could want, smart and successful.

In 1956 I took a leave of absence from the Post Office and Florence and I took the girls to Australia to meet her side of the family. We picked up a drive-away car in Dallas and motored up through Colorado and Utah, then on through Lake Tahoe to San Francisco, where we were to board our ship. It was a station wagon, so there was plenty of room for four active children.

We were driving across the Oakland Bay Bridge. Vicki Lynn, who was in her second year of school, was sitting behind me looking out the window at a car in the next lane, when she called out, "Look, Daddy, look! There's Chineses!"

I glanced to my left. There was a car full of Asians. Chinese or Japanese, I didn't know which. Instantly this cold chill came over me. They were the first I'd seen since the war.

We stayed in Australia ten months. The Australians are great people. They had three jobs waiting for me when we arrived. They made us feel welcome. But in the end, we came home, to the United States.

For thirty-five years I pushed the war out of my mind. I never talked about it to anyone, period. There were two or three Marines that worked down at the Post Office. Sometimes we'd joke about the funny things that had happened. But we never really talked about the war. I just held it all back.

In 1979, I got a phone call. Stumpy Stanley, our old company commander, Bill Leyden and a few others from the First Marine Division had been sitting in a New York bar having a drink. One of them said, "We should get everybody together again." Before they split up, each promised to call other Marines he knew from the war and pass the word along. When the call came around to me, I started calling the guys I knew. I'd kept up with Jim Burke, of course. He was living in Clinton, Iowa. I remembered John Redifer lived in Portland, Oregon. Marmet lived in Ohio. Tom Matheney lived in Monterey, Tennessee. When I didn't know their number, I called information. And so it went until I'd found twelve people.

In 1980 twenty of us from K Company went to the Marine Association First Division reunion in Indianapolis. Gene Sledge was there, Mo Darsey, our old gunny sergeant. Johnny Marmet. Tom Matheney. The whole crowd. Guys I had spent months and even years with, guys I had fought alongside.

We'd sit around and talk. One of them would say, "Hey, Burgin, do you remember the day such-and-such happened?"

I'd say, "No, I don't remember that."

And they'd say, "You ought to. You were there."

They'd talk about how this happened, how that happened. Go into details about what went on. I'd just sit there.

Then, all of a sudden it would flash through my mind, and I could see it again as plain as day.

I started attending the reunions every year after that.

At the 1983 reunion, Stumpy Stanley said to me, "I talked to Jim Kornaizl the other day. He said to tell you hello."

"Who? You talked to who?"

"Jim Kornaizl."

"I don't know a Jim Kornaizl."

"He sure knows you. That's for sure."

It bugged me after that that I could not recall Jim Kornaizl. The next year, 1984, we held our reunion in Milwaukee.

A guy was coming down the hallway toward me in the hotel. The moment I saw him, it all came back. The flash of the shell. He and T. L. Hudson on the ground, wounded, and Kornaizl twitching from head to foot.

Why I had put that out of my head I do not know. I had remembered Hudson getting hit. But not Kornaizl.

We talked for a while. He had spent eighteen months in the hospital. They had put a steel plate in his skull, and when he started having convulsions again they opened him up and cleaned it out and put in another steel plate.

Within a few years I got to the point where I could talk about the war any time, any place, with anybody. It got me thinking: This needs to be told, what we went through.

Florence and I had the air-conditioner man out to the house the other day for a little preseason maintenance. He was looking at the pictures on my wall, at my KA-BAR in its frame, at the flag and the Bronze Star I got in 1946.

I asked him if he'd ever heard of Peleliu.

No, he'd never heard of Peleliu.

I didn't figure he had. I told him we'd had sixty-five hundred casualties in thirty days on that little island. I didn't tell him about the flies and the maggots and the rot, the bad water and heat and caves, about how you never knew where the next bullet was going to come from.

The big famous battles—Iwo Jima, Guadalcanal, Okinawa. Everybody's heard about them. Nobody's heard of Peleliu. They don't teach history anymore.

So I made up my mind to teach it. There's only a few of us left who know anything about Peleliu. When we started our reunions we had 250 on our roster. Now we're down to forty. We lost five since our last reunion. Only a few of us are left who remember. We have to tell the stories, so this and future generations will know what happened. So it doesn't get forgotten.

———

What sticks with me now is not so much the pain and terror and sorrow of the war, though I remember that well enough. What really sticks with me is the honor I had of defending my country, and of serving in the company of these men. They were good Marines, the finest, every one of them. You can't say anything better about a man.

Semper Fi!

Selected Bibliography

OVERVIEWS

Costello, John. *The Pacific War 1941–1945.* Perennial/HarperCollins, New York City, 1981.

Dear, I. C. B., general editor, and Foot, M. R. D., consultant editor. *The Oxford Companion to World War II.* Oxford University Press, Oxford, England, 1995.

Hammel, Eric. *Pacific Warriors: The U.S. Marines in World War II, A Pictorial Tribute.* Zenith Press/MBI Publishing Company, St. Paul, Minnesota, 2005.

McMillan, George. *The Old Breed: A History of the First Marine Division in World War II.* Zenger Publishing Company, Washington, D.C., 1949/1979.

Rottman, Gordon L. *U.S. Marine Rifleman 1939–1945.* Warrior Series #112. Osprey Publishing, Midway House, West Way, Botley, Oxford, England, 2006.

NEW BRITAIN AND CAPE GLOUCESTER

Bielakowski, Alexander M. "New Britain" in *World War II in the Pacific: An Encyclopedia.* Garland Publishing, Inc. New York City, 2001.

Hough, Major Frank O., USMCR, and Major John A. Crown, USMCR. *The Campaign on New Britain.* Historic Division, Headquarters, U.S. Marine Corps, Washington, D.C., 1952.

Miller, John, Jr. *Cartwheel: The Reduction of Rabaul.* United States Army in World War II. Office of the Chief of Military History, Department of the Army, Washington, D.C., 1959.

Nalty, Bernard C. *Cape Gloucester: The Green Inferno.* Marines in World War II Commemorative Series. Marine Corps Historical Center, Washington, D.C., 1994.

PELELIU AND PAVUVU

A&E Television Networks. *Our Century: The Bloody Hills of Peleliu.* The History Channel, 1995 (DVD).

Camp, Dick. *The Last Man Standing: The 1st Marine Regiment on Peleliu, September 15–21, 1944.* Zenith Press/MBI Publishing Co. Minneapolis, Minnesota, 2008.

DeHart, Bruce. "Palau" in *World War II in the Pacific: An Encyclopedia.* Garland Publishing, Inc. New York City, 2001.

Faith, William Robert. *Bob Hope: A Life in Comedy.* G. P. Putnam's Sons, New York City, 1982.

Hallas, James H. *The Devil's Anvil: The Assault on Peleliu.* Praeger, Westport, Connecticut, 1994.

Hope, Bob, with Linda Hope. *My Life in Jokes.* Hyperion, New York City, 2003.

Hough, Major Frank O., USMCR. *The Assault on Peleliu.* Historic Division, Headquarters, U.S. Marine Corps, Washington, D.C., 1950; reprint: The Battery Press, Inc., Nashville, Tennessee, 2000.

MacMillan, George. "They Called It a Rest Camp: The First Marine Division on Pavuvu." *Harper's,* October, 1949, pp. 36–45.

Moran, Jim, and Gordon L. Rottman. *Peleliu 1944: The Forgotten Corner of Hell.* Campaign Series #110. Osprey Publishing, New York City, 2002.

Phillips, Sidney C., M.D. *"You'll Be Sor-ree!"* Artcraft Press, Mobile, Alabama, 2001.

Pollins, Perry. *Tales of a Feather Merchant: The World War II Memoir of a Marine Radioman.* Merriam Press, Bennington, Vermont, 2008.

Sledge, E. B. *With the Old Breed at Peleliu and Okinawa.* Ballantine Books, New York City, 2007.

Wright, Derrick. *To the Far Side of Hell: The Battle for Peleliu, 1944.* University of Alabama Press, Tuscaloosa, Alabama, 2005.

OKINAWA

Leckie, Robert. *Okinawa: The Last Battle of World War II.* Viking Penguin, New York City, 1996.

Rottman, Gordon. *Okinawa 1945: The Last Battle.* Praeger Illustrated Military History Series, Praeger Publishers, Westport, Connecticut, 2002.

Sloan, Bill. *The Ultimate Battle: Okinawa 1945—The Last Epic Struggle of World War II.* Simon & Schuster, New York City, 2007.

Index

Forty-sixth Replacement Battalion, 103
Fourth Marine Division, 202
Fouts, Peter, 199
Friendly fire, 15, 73, 74, 137, 148–49
Friendship School, Jewett, 22

Geglein, Andrew, 90
Geiger, Roy S., 98, 260
Gentian violet, 84
Goannas, 201–2
Goodenough Island, 66
Grable, Betty, 199
Grasshoppers (*see* Spotter planes)
Great Depression, 26, 276
Guadalcanal, 47, 49–50, 52, 57–58, 75, 76, 98,
    103, 110, 117, 118, 121, 155, 181, 191,
    201–3, 285
Guam, 110, 117, 177, 202
Gustafson, John, 141, 216

Haldane, Andrew Allison "Ack-Ack," 111–12,
    145, 146, 149, 168, 183, 192, 264
    death of, 180–81
Halsey, William F. "Bull," 127
Hammocks, 83, 99
Haney, Elmo, 106, 139
Hankins, Joseph, 177–78
Hara-kiri, 90–91, 262
Harris, Harold "Bucky," 176
Hayes, Gabby, 254
Hellcat fighters, 122, 144, 214
Henderson Field, Guadalcanal, 203
Hendricks, Ted, 195
Higgins boats, 5, 6, 117, 169, 184, 190,
    203–4, 214
Hill 55, Okinawa, 250
Hill 100, Peleliu, 170
Hill 100A, Peleliu, 170
Hill 120, Peleliu, 170
Hill 140, Peleliu, 170, 179, 182
Hill 150, New Britain, 77
Hill 660, New Britain, 81
Hip pocket artillery, 48
Hizoanna, Okinawa, 222
Holiday celebrations, 198–200
Honolulu, 49
Hope, Bob, 114–16
Horseshoe, Peleliu, 169–70, 176,
    179–80, 182
Howard, Lonnie, 4–5, 79

Hudson, T. L. "Peaches," 192, 198, 203, 240,
    277, 280, 284
Hull, Ed, 26–27

In Old Oklahoma (movie), 254
Iwo Jima, 121, 202, 285

Japanese aircraft, 76–77, 88, 205, 207,
    212–14, 219–20, 227, 228
Japanese main islands, 201, 204, 205
Jewett, Texas, 22, 275, 276
Jones, Edward A. "Hillbilly," 108–10, 112, 113,
    120, 138, 139–41, 183, 189, 216, 264
    death of, 178, 179, 181
Jungle juice, 198
Jungle rot, 84, 93

K Company Mortars (K/3/5)
    on New Britain, 4, 11, 12, 71–93, 99, 135,
        143, 219, 227
    on Ngesebus, 155–69, 181, 184, 236
    on Okinawa, 204–5, 207, 208, 214–36,
        239–52, 255–64
    on Pavuvu, 97–111, 114–17, 132, 133, 143,
        169, 189–201
    on Peleliu, 3, 5–17, 31, 51, 127–52, 155–59,
        162, 167, 169–85, 202, 208, 215, 217,
        227, 230, 236, 258, 284–85
    reunions of, 283–85
    on Takabanare, 226, 236
    on Talasea, 86–87, 93, 120
Kadena airfield, Okinawa, 218
Kamikaze attacks, 220
Katz, Wesley, 251, 252
Kehoe, R. F., Jr., 16
Knee mortars, 9, 85, 89
Korean War, 22
Kornaizl, Jim, 240, 283–84
Kunishi Ridge, Okinawa, 258–60
Kwajalein, 114, 202
Kyushu, 205, 217

Land crabs, 83–84, 99–100, 116, 190, 246
Langford, Frances, 114
LCIs (Landing Craft, Infantry), 201
LCMs, 85, 93
Legs, Lieutenant, 15–16, 92–93, 106–8, 160,
    194, 243
Lewis, William, 165, 166
Leyden, Bill, 282